Praise for *The Asylum Seekers*

"This book is a cleric's account of her sojourn among people camped at our country's southern border, people seeking asylum and rarely receiving it. Rathbone writes with admirable candor about her small triumphs and failures, her doubts and uncertainties. But to me, the great strength of this story is the author's passionate sympathy for the desperate people she works with. It suffuses the book, like antivenin to the slanders forever thrown at immigrants."

—**Tracy Kidder**, Pulitzer Prize–winning author of *Rough Sleepers* and *Mountains Beyond Mountains*

"*The Asylum Seekers* shines with a kind of moral clarity that illuminates not only the horrific effects of the United States immigration system on individuals, families, and children, but the personal toll of working alongside those affected. A must-read for those hoping to understand the border on a human level."

—**Alejandra Oliva**, author of *Rivermouth: A Chronicle of Language Faith and Migration*

"Cristina Rathbone's new book *The Asylum Seekers*, her deeply observed account of time at the border, is elegant, unsentimental, loving, and piercingly honest. It is a prayer—and almost a miracle. Not because prayer is magic, but because it is the planting ground for hope. For those who despair and those who rage, for all who thirst, Cristina Rathbone digs a furrow in the dirt of our shared suffering, and makes a space where we can abide together."

—**Sara Miles**, author of *Take This Bread* and *City of God*

"No other book I've read brings you so closely, so intimately, into the lives of Latin American migrants living in poverty, most of whom are humble families with children. Fleeing horrors and lethal danger, they encounter the new horrors of US border policies bent on ending the right to asylum. Cristina Rathbone's initial sense of helplessness leads to a profound and painful, yet finally inspiring interrogation into the meaning of her faith. Drawing strength from the migrants, in heartbreak and suffering so patiently endured, in so much human love and innocence, she discovers the resourcefulness and courage that lead to some of the most rousing episodes of this powerfully written book. At moments, *The Asylum Seekers* seems to combine the genres of the thriller and the account of a pilgrim's progress. This staggeringly beautiful and important book will fill your heart and mind with a sense of wonder, sorrow, and gratitude for what it has shown you."

—**Francisco Goldman**, Pulitzer Prize–finalist author of *Monkey Boy* and *Say Her Name*

"A wise pastor once told me that genuine ministry means getting 'between the marrow and bone' of human experience. As both a priest and an author, Cristina Rathbone has more than answered that sacred summons in her book about the families herded and penned along the US-Mexico border, literally within sight of the asylum they so desperately seek. These pages are filled with both anguish and uplift, and they depict a religious faith that is anything but ethereal. Nothing I have read about the so-called border crisis has torn up my heart and haunted my conscience like *The Asylum Seekers*."

—**Samuel G. Freedman**, award-winning author of *Upon This Rock* and *Into the Bright Sunshine*

"Cristina Rathbone is the rare spiritual memoirist who also has the descriptive gifts of a reporter. With *The Asylum Seekers*, she brings to life the beauty, kinship, and compassion of individuals seeking asylum at the US-Mexico border and the often insurmountable obstacles they must face. A vivid and searing look at one of the most important stories of our time."

— **Stephanie Saldaña**, author of *What We Remember Will Be Saved*

"This a book on the edge, by a priest on the edge. The Paso del Norte bridge at the US–Mexico border is both a physical structure and a moral faultline. In *The Asylum Seekers*, Cristina Rathbone submits herself, body and soul, to the teaching of the people who most clearly see its double nature: the powerless, the victimized, the dispossessed and exploited. Taking nothing for granted, and with a style that clicks like a Geiger counter at the approach of primary reality, Rathbone crosses frontier after frontier of understanding. What if poverty of spirit were the secret to great journalism?"

—**James Parker**, *Atlantic* staff writer and author of *Get Me Through the Next Five Minutes*

"What an exceptional book this is—heart-rending, heart-opening, and impossible to put down. Part brilliant reportage, part thrilling spiritual narrative, this extraordinary account of time spent among the desperate and neglected families on the US–Mexico border will convince you that no real spirituality is complete if it's not socially engaged. Urgent, necessary, beautifully written—an essential book for our times."

—**Henry Shukman**, author of *One Blade of Grass* and *Original Love*

"With the eloquence of a poet, the spiritual depth of a contemplative, and the courage of a prophet, Cristina Rathbone reveals to us the faces of the immigrants who live and die on the borderland. As she notes, today that borderland crosses not only the Rio Grande but every street and neighborhood of our land. With unrelenting honesty, Rathbone likewise reveals how her encounters with the men, women, and children seeking asylum break open her own heart in ways she could never have imagined. She reminds us that the most revolutionary—and most Christian—of all human acts is the simple yet seemingly 'useless' act of being fully present and attentive to another human being in their suffering. When we do that, we discover that resurrection is not what happens after crucifixion, but in its very midst. And we learn that we will be resurrected together or not at all."

—**Roberto Goizueta**, Margaret O'Brien Flatley Professor Emeritus of Catholic Theology at Boston College; author of *Caminemos con Jesús*

"*The Asylum Seekers* is an honest, compelling, and heartfelt journey into the death-dealing realities occasioned by the United States' actions on its border with Mexico. Cristina Rathbone movingly portrays the dignity, grace, and strength of those seeking asylum and a better, safer life in the United States. She shares the incarnate reality of her story and the stories of women, men, and children with whom she lives and works on the border. This is an uplifting tale of faith, hope, and life in the midst of despair, evil, and death. Read it and be moved."

—**Ian Douglas**, author and retired Episcopal bishop of Connecticut

THE ASYLUM SEEKERS

THE ASYLUM SEEKERS

A CHRONICLE OF LIFE, DEATH, AND COMMUNITY AT THE BORDER

Cristina Rathbone

Broadleaf Books
Minneapolis

THE ASYLUM SEEKERS
A Chronicle of Life, Death, and Community at the Border

Copyright © 2025 Cristina Rathbone. Published by Broadleaf Books. All rights reserved. Except for brief quotations in critical articles or reviews, no part of this book may be reproduced in any manner without prior written permission from the publisher. Email copyright@broadleafbooks.com or write to Permissions, Broadleaf Books, PO Box 1209, Minneapolis, MN 55440-1209.

29 28 27 26 25 24   1 2 3 4 5 6 7 8 9

The names of asylum seekers and Border Patrol officers have been changed to protect their privacy.

Library of Congress Cataloging-in-Publication Data

Names: Rathbone, Cristina, author.
Title: The asylum seekers : a chronicle of life, death, and community at the Border / Cristina Rathbone.
Description: Minneapolis : Broadleaf Books, [2025] | Includes bibliographical references.
Identifiers: LCCN 2024020488 (print) | LCCN 2024020489 (ebook) | ISBN 9798889832010 (hardcover) | ISBN 9798889832027 (ebook)
Subjects: LCSH: Immigrants—Mexican American Border Region—Social conditions. | Immigrants—Mexican American Border Region—Religious life. | Noncitizens—Mexican American Border Region—Social conditions. | Noncitizens—Mexican American Border Region—Religious life. | Faith. | Mexico—Emigration and immigration—Government policy. | United States—Emigration and immigration—Government policy.
Classification: LCC JV7403 .R38 2025 (print) | LCC JV7403 (ebook) | DDC 305.9/0691209721—dc23/eng/20240722
LC record available at https://lccn.loc.gov/2024020488
LC ebook record available at https://lccn.loc.gov/2024020489

Cover image: /1675822168 by satika
Cover design: Faceout Studio

Print ISBN: 979-8-8898-3201-0
eBook ISBN: 979-8-8898-3202-7

Printed in China.

As long as there are people, Christ will walk the earth as your neighbor, as the one through whom God calls you, speaks to you, makes demands on you.

—Dietrich Bonhoeffer

For Jack and Lucas

INTRODUCTION

WHEN I FIRST arrived on the border, I had just left a congregation of unhoused people with whom I'd started a faith community in Boston. I'd worked with the men and women who lived largely on the street—"the brick," they called it—for almost twelve years, had found a real home with them, and felt alive in ways that were real and true and expanding. I loved my work and relied on the community to teach and form and shape me, both as a person and as a priest.

But for three years, stories of the border had been besieging us all. Children stripped from their parents and put in cages. Dead parents clinging to dead children on the banks of border rivers. Boatloads of people—men, women, and children—drowning in the Adriatic and the Mediterranean. Thousands walking for days and then weeks and then months through the muddy fields and crumbling, gray towns of Eastern Europe. Newly militarized borders around the world were slamming shut everywhere: in California and Arizona and Texas and France and Italy and Poland and Greece. Across the globe, more people were on the move than at any time since World War II.

During a brief trip to visit my mother in London, I'd snuck across the channel to France to visit the Church of England's first-ever refugee chaplain in Calais and saw there how migrants' tents were slashed to shreds—not by thugs or gang members but by orderly groups of uniformed police officers. Gas stations close to the channel were housed in 3D wire mesh cages as they were the places, people said, that migrants were most likely to break into the backs of trucks, or scramble onto their undercarriages, or squeeze onto their roofs in their attempts to get across the water to the United Kingdom. The highways leading up to the coast were fenced in this way too—strips of four-lane tarmac stretched between tall barbed-wire fences, the entire network of roads as fenced off from the surrounding countryside as a militarized airport.

This was surreal, of course. And horrifying. And almost impossible to take in. But in one way, at least, none of it seemed new to me. My mother's family is Cuban, and every one of my aunts and uncles and cousins and grandparents left what they knew for new lives in the States. I'd grown up on stories of Cubans in tiny makeshift boats and oversized inner tubes, setting out from the beaches of the northern coast of the island, never to be seen again. In my mother's small flat in London, there was always hung a bright array of painted wooden plaques, and framed colored drawings, and papier-mâché statues of Cuba's patron saint, La Virgen del Cobre. Hovering in yellow robes above tiny people crammed into fragile-looking boats in an angry sea, she offered protection to all those waving their arms in the air in the universal signal of distress.

When I was nineteen, I headed out for a walk before breakfast one morning in Miami and came across a freshly washed-up boat on the beach, lying off kilter in the curly, black seaweed. It was a small white and gray boat, open to the elements, with nothing in it but a few scraps of brightly colored material, empty plastic bottles tied together with string, and, right in the middle, a squat tent made of canvas, under which sat a bulky, square engine. "A lawnmower engine they used!" my uncle exclaimed in Spanish as he and four other elderly Cuban men clambered over the boat like crabs. "You see that?" he marveled. "It's a lawnmower engine!" This was the only thing anyone said. Otherwise, we were silent. Hushed. The boat had made it, but it was empty: a not quite yet acknowledged tomb. Who'd been in it? This was our silent question. And had there been children? The men looked silently for signs.

About ten minutes later, three shirtless young men came limping up the beach. Yes, yes, it was their boat, they said, exulting through cracked lips. And yes, they'd come from Cuba, though they must have been blown off course, because it had taken them four days to cross the ninety-mile passage to Florida. Four days? the old men marveled. Yes. Four days and four nights, they said. But now—what was this?—they simply couldn't understand it! They'd walked for miles down the beach and could find no way off it into the town that wasn't barred by fences and tall, locked metal gates. Such is life in America, the old men told them, filled with wonder at these young men's fortitude and pride of their own hard-won knowledge of the system—and, most of all, of having, for once, the literal key to get them in.

Old men wrapped arms around young men then, leading them down the beach to their apartments, promising places to stay and connections to work. And as I turned to leave, one of the young ones, the one with curly hair now matted flat against his skull and deep white cuts along his lips, turned to me and winked. "Oye, chica," he said, eyes sparking as if we were meeting in a nightclub, "¿quieres salir conmigo?"

There's so much to say about all this—too much for now. The point here is only that people who fled from one country to another, and stuck together, and made new lives for themselves even as they upheld the old way of living and talking and eating and drinking and dancing—all with a just-below-the-surface conviction in their own superiority, which Anglos always seemed to miss—for me, this was normal. This was life. The courage and stamina and raw, we-will-not-only-manage-but-thrive approach to life's difficulties were all to be admired and, if possible, emulated.

No surprise, then, that when it came time to leave the homeless community in Boston, I headed for the US-Mexico border. Like the young men on the boat that day, my family was given the benefit of the doubt when they arrived in this country. They were given a chance. But by 2019, US immigration policies were being shaped not to assist but to crush people just like those I love more than anyone in the world. I needed to go see what I could do—or, better, what we could do together. And to do that, of course, I needed to learn from the only people who could really teach me: the migrants and refugees and asylum seekers themselves.

More than this, however, I didn't know. Where would I work? With whom? And to what specific end? I had no idea. I raised enough money to last six months and tried to leave it at that.

The story that follows traces just one part of this work: four short months spent on a single block of a single street at the foot of a single port of entry into the States from Mexico. I'd been on the border for close to five months by the time this story starts, and the experiences I'd learned about—and, in some small cases, shared in—informed and deepened my time with the people on this street. But the truth is that I still had no real idea what I was doing. And this feeling never left me. I felt it keenly even on my last day there as I walked back across the Paso del Norte bridge into El Paso from Juárez for the very last time.

I mention this now, openly and up front, because I've come to believe that this pervasive not knowing—this conscious and unending sense of partial lostness—is essential to any real, on-the-ground work with people whose suffering is both extreme and long-lasting. It is only when we know that we don't know, after all, that we most genuinely seek. And it is when we genuinely seek that we are most deeply found, by each other and also by God.

And this is the other reason I went to the border—less easy to trace, perhaps, but no less elemental than the way I am made: I needed God palpable in my life again, manifest and visible and sturdy enough to wallop me back into sanity and truth from the meandering paths of self on which I waste so much time.

I did not go to the border as a journalist, though I'd spent most of my adult life working as one before I was ordained a priest in the Episcopal Church at the age of forty-three. Nor did I go there as a social activist or a political organizer. Big ideas and muscular, courageous policies are essential if we are ever to wrest justice from the maw of horror that is our immigration system today. I pray every day for the leaders and thinkers and organizers who do this work. But I am not one of them. In fact, I am the opposite: give me an ideal and give me an individual, and I'll choose the individual every time—which, in part, is why I stopped being a journalist and started being a priest.

This book offers nothing like an objective or a comprehensive account of the border, then. It is far more personal than that, far more ephemeral. Instead, what follows is a collection of stories about myself, and the border, and a handful of people who tried to survive there, even as they sought something more. And it is also, I pray, a story about God: not as God is so often portrayed, tucked away in the corner of a pretty church someplace, or floating, disembodied, above the fray, but of God enfleshed and incarnate, out in the heart of the suffering world—*with* and *as* and *in* the people who wait so vulnerably there.

God is not often spoken about in this way, I know. Humanity either. And I think I get why. It is easier—cleaner, simpler, far more readily comprehensible—to place us *here* and God *there* as if we were entirely separate entities, responsive to each other, certainly, but distinct and ever apart. This makes sense in a way. And perhaps it is better than nothing. But I can't help but think that this way of looking at things makes a kind of gruel of the feast that is actually given us. Day-to-day life, with the power of the divine strained out of it, lacks the heft of a more integrated reality—and it lacks the hope too. It is as if, in the name of God, we religious professionals too often do the opposite of what we are supposed to do. We strip a full dimension out of life as it actually is right here and right now, only to put it in a bottle to distribute later, with a pipette, in carefully measured drops. My hope is in part to correct for this tendency. I fail, I know, far more often than I succeed, but it still feels important to try.

I came to religion late in life, well into adulthood, which perhaps skews my vision. But even before I stumbled into a church in my mid-thirties, I sensed that the depths and the height of the world could be found buried deep in the heart of us all.

I was a journalist back then, as I've said, and had spent years writing about unhoused folks and women in prison and kids posturing in gangs or left alone to hawk dime bags of smack on the corner—and I'd seen it in them, this immeasurable beauty and power. Lose focus for a second and I'd miss it, of course. But when I paid enough attention and dared remain open to the horror and the beauty and the pain and the brokenness—whoosh!—there it was, flashing out and then dimming, cratering in and then covering: the ground of us all that was life.

I had no way to understand this back then or to contextualize it even. All I knew was that this ground or core or energy or life was shared by us all and that it was most often visible out beyond the muffling confines of comfort, in the places of poverty and suffering and injustice. There, stripped of pretense and protection, it was as if we were all at least occasionally forced into being who we actually were, in our essence. And that essence was the point. Sometimes it seemed very dark and sometimes bright as a flare, but always it felt sacred and powerful and inextinguishable. And it was part of what had kept me going back to the corner, or the cell, or the brick because it was there that I got to spend time with people who knew its truth too.

Then, one rainy morning about twenty years ago, I walked into a church for the funeral of the spouse of a colleague. There I found it again—that same essence or power or life—palpable as the great clouds of incense that were pluming their way through the silence to the ceiling. I was completely astonished by this, utterly taken aback. It had been decades since I'd been in a church, and I had no interest in organized religion of any kind at all. Yet there it was, indisputable, this core of life that I'd only ever seen in people who were suffering, visibly filling the space to the rafters.

I snuck back to that same church the following Sunday, and the Sunday after that, and the Sunday after that one too. And the stories I began to hear there—stories about a God who became human, only to be shunned and blamed and arrested and ultimately executed—so precisely overlaid the stories of the people I wrote about that they offered me, for the first time in my life, both an explanation and a name for the power, beauty, and sheer, blinding life force I had so often encountered in them: *Emmanuel*, they called it. *God with us.*

Emmanuel. It is the name given to the little one born in poverty and peril on a border of another kind, who came to show us how to become who we already are. And it is what hope means for me too. And purpose. And possibility. And it is everywhere; that's the thing: everywhere and always and available to all with no sign-up fees or requirements of any kind at all—except a certain kind of poverty, which, at least for me, is almost impossible to truly desire, even as I know it is the key to the only door that makes us truly free.

I know all this must sound both pious and vague—forgive me. If I could put it any more clearly, I would never have had to write the words that follow. Best to stick with Jesus, then. Here's how he put it in the most important teaching of his too short life. Clear, simple, and directly to the point:

Blessed are the poor . . . for theirs is the kingdom of heaven.

1

I'D BEEN IN Ciudad Juárez for just three weeks when the first Mexican asylum seekers arrived at the border. I turned left off the bridge between downtown El Paso and downtown Juárez as I always had, heading east to the huge, white tent to which asylum seekers were returned each day from immigration detention centers across the Rio Grande in the United States. As I walked, I saw a large group of people gathered in front of the pistachio-colored Michoacána ice cream store. They looked disheveled, as if they'd spent the night, and I walked past, strangely nervous, wondering whether it was possible for a homeless community to spring up so suddenly.

The rest of the day I did as I'd done for weeks: I handed out water and fresh snacks in the tent that volunteers had erected to welcome and care for the hundreds of asylum seekers who were forcibly returned from the United States each day. By the following morning, though, the crowd in front of the ice cream store had doubled. Perhaps a hundred men, women, and children were gathered there now, and they'd definitely spent the night. Flattened cardboard boxes, clearly used to sleep on, were neatly leaned against walls behind little piles of gear up and down the street.

Something was going on, I realized—something new and strange. On my way home from the tent, I stopped at the green paletería, bought an ice cream, and then leaned up against a pillar as I ate it, watching and listening and getting a feel.

There was a bus stop across the street, and I wondered for a moment if that could be why all these people were gathered. But a huge yellow bus wheezed to a halt in front of it a few minutes later, and six or seven well-dressed people who looked nothing like the newly arrived crowd got on. No one there now was waiting for a bus.

There were lots of children, whole families, and up and down the street, kids were crouched on tightly packed, brightly colored book bags, staring at nothing. Small groups of women were gathered together in clumps, talking so quietly to each other that they had to lean in close to be heard. Everything on the block felt suspended, at once agitated and paused.

After a time, I asked a man standing next to me if he knew anything about what was going on. Keeping his eyes fixed straight ahead of him, he nodded once and then said yes in that drawn-out way Mexicans use to suggest layers upon layers of meaning, too many for words: "Si—i—i—i . . ." Then, after a long pause, a hovering, he turned to me: "We are here because of the bridge," he said. "We are Mexicans seeking asylum."

Before that first day, I'd grown almost accustomed to the weird simplicity of walking across a bridge to leave one country and enter another. Each morning, I had my fifty cents ready, knowing this was what it cost to leave the country on the US side. I knew to smile and offer a casual half-wave toward the heavily armed Mexican National Guard members on the other side, too, down by Juárez Avenue, where the sidewalks of the bridge gave out into the pulsing, dusty vibrancy of downtown. I knew that the intersection where the bridge and Juárez met held a twice-life-sized, bright-pink wooden cross at its center, encircled by hundreds of rusted nails sticking out at all angles, both defense and offense, like a porcupine. I knew that pink crosses themselves were a symbol of resistance and remembrance in that city, where so many women had been killed that the term *feminicidio*, "femicide," had been coined to differentiate the often brutally disfiguring murders of women from the thousands of others—which, when combined, made Juárez the fifth most dangerous city in the world. I knew how many asylum seekers there were in the city, which US policies most affected them, and who was most able to help. I even knew a couple of extraordinary "retired" priests and nuns, both Catholic and Episcopal, who were generous enough to show me around.

But I still had no real understanding of the border. Perhaps I still don't. Perhaps the border is as impossible to know in any kind of fixed or permanent way as a river. Or perhaps I left before I found solid ground under all that movement and resistance and change. I don't know.

What I do know is that I didn't yet understand how unusual it was to see large groups of asylum seekers hanging around the downtown Juárez port of entry. Before I arrived in Juárez, I'd been in Tijuana, the far western edge of the US-Mexico border, which backs up against the Pacific. There in Tijuana, three or four hundred asylum seekers from across the world gathered at the port of entry before dawn every day, just around the corner from the gate where those of us with US passports or legal visas crossed into the States. There they waited and watched and jostled toward a lone Mexican official, who sleepily governed the chaos from a foldout card table in the small patch of shade cast by the only tree on the block.

The process in Juárez, however, was more orderly. Here, officials regulating asylum seekers' access to the border did so out of a sprawling one-story building just a block from the bridge, and in place of the single official with his card table under a tree, uniformed men and women from a variety of organizations managed access to the US checkpoint with relative efficiency.

This meant, in part, that except during the daily cross-border rush between six and eight in the morning, when a long, slow-moving but orderly line of pedestrians waiting to enter the States to work or study or visit family or shop sometimes spilled out from the bridge onto Juárez Avenue, the downtown area was at least relatively free from the crowded chaos of other border crossings I'd seen. Instead, the blocks surrounding the downtown port of entry catered primarily not to desperate migrants fleeing for their lives but to US tourists visiting Mexico for pleasure, or cut-price health care, or even a meal or a night on the town. Currency exchanges, affordable dentists, and discount pharmacies lined the avenue on both sides, along with cowboy boot and trinket stores, restaurants, bars, and, just a block or two to the west, hookers of every kind.

This is not to say that Juárez wasn't as full of desperate migrants seeking access to the States as every other city on the southern side of the border, because it was. In the second half of 2019, more than seventeen thousand officially registered asylum seekers were stuck in the city. But they were largely tucked away in airplane hangar–sized shelters or in little hotels and smaller faith-based centers half an hour or more by car across the sprawling city from the border. In part because the city was so dangerous—especially but not exclusively for poor travelers far from home—most kept away from the border until they were summoned.

The following day, as I again turned left off the bridge to make my way to the tent, the crowd on the street with the ice cream store seemed to have doubled yet again. I slowed my pace, lingering first with a man by the chiclet stand on the corner, then with a group of kids playing soccer with a more or less rounded stone one of them had just pulled from the dirt at the edge of the sidewalk, and finally settled in with a young mother, Gabriela, and her kids—Javier, Ana, and six-week-old baby Carlos.

It was very hot that day—109 degrees, my phone told me when I checked—and the sun felt sharp like a weapon. Sitting down with Gabriela, the kids, and the baby on the yellow plastic poncho she had spread out on the sidewalk, I experienced again that mysterious process of dropping through the fast-paced, work-a-day world into the slower, more spacious realm of those with no place to go. Above us, people walked past on their way to work, or to the store, or to the port of entry with all the closed-off urgency of people in cities everywhere, while on the sidewalk six-year-old Luz shared a red lollipop with the baby, tracing his lips with it back and forth, back and forth, letting him suck.

They had arrived by bus from Zacatecas the day before, Gabriela told me. Apart from her brother, who'd stayed behind, this was all that was left of her family—except, she said in the most skipping-over-it kind of way, her husband, who was dead now anyway, she thought, murdered, though his body had never turned up the way so many others had, heavily mutilated and in parts. "I am scared they will come and find us here," she told me, smiling as if willing me to dissuade her of this, to tell her she was crazy. Then four-year-old Javier charged after something in the street, and she shouted out his name, "Javier! *Javier!*" until he came back, dragging his feet, reluctant to be hemmed in again with his mother on the sidewalk.

Slowly, between long stretches of exhausted silence, Gabriela explained how she'd been told that this violence against her husband would get her and the children into the States. This is what her neighbors had said, she told me, and then again: yes, this is what they said. Now, though, she was thinking maybe no. She'd gone up to the checkpoint at the top of the bridge just like everyone else when she'd first arrived, and she had tried to explain her situation to the officials. But they had refused to let her show them the photos or to say much of anything at all. They told her only, she said, that they didn't have room. That she should try again later. That maybe then there would be space.

She'd had no idea at all it would be like this, she said when I asked. Pues, of course she didn't! Would she have brought the children and the little baby all this way if she did? Embarrassed by the clumsiness of my question, I bought some snacks from a street vendor then, and we spent the next few minutes eating fresh-fried potato chips dripping with lime and hot sauce out of transparent plastic bags. After that I held the baby for a bit and chatted with Luz and with Javier, and later, bolstering herself, Gabriela said that the days had not really been so bad. The other women on the street had been kind to her, she said, and the kids had already started to play with others down the block where the sidewalk widened out. But the night had been . . . well, the night had been . . . pues, the night had been very hard. It was frightening sleeping—just like this!—on the sidewalk, especially with the babies. And this morning, she told me, smiling as if embarrassed, the children were complaining their backs hurt from sleeping on the concrete.

I'd been on the border as a kind of untethered and roving priest for five months by then, traveling on my own from town to town, meeting people, listening, learning, praying, and then trying to make sense of it all. I went with no real plan and was connected directly to no one diocese, or team, or office, which left me free to volunteer with agencies of all kinds up and down the border. This freedom had felt essential back in Boston, where I lived. I'd long been lodged there in the heart of a large and vibrant faith community made up largely of people experiencing homelessness, but that community had grown through relationships that had developed slowly, one by one, over years. To begin with, and for months, I'd simply walked around, settling in under an alcove with someone for an afternoon or helping someone else carry their bags two at a time, from their daytime spot to their evening spot. The larger, more formal, and regular gatherings of the community had grown slowly, organically, and in response to the particular needs of those particular people in that particular place.

I was not a believer in ready-made, replicable "ministries," is what I am trying to say, and had insisted that if we wanted to start something new on the border, the first step had to be spending real time with the people who were there. Only they really knew what was needed, I told my superiors whenever they asked for a more concrete plan, and only with and through them could a small, real ministry grow.

I did what I could to prepare before leaving Boston, of course. After finishing work with the homeless community downtown, I spent hours at home reading and making calls and writing emails and praying and even sitting on the cold, stone floor of a monastery chapel I loved, between services, when the space was empty and dark. There I tried to locate the clarity and peace that I knew was there but could not seem to access whenever I asked: What responsibility does having an American passport actually hold? And how can I, both as a human being and as a priest, make the most of the privileges it grants?

I wrote to priests and deacons and bishops up and down the border and registered for a multi-diocese conference planned for November in Arizona, which only made me panic—a conference in seven months' time was not enough to be going on.

In the end, I simply gave up trying to create anything like a coherent plan; called an old friend in Mexico; invited myself to stay; then packed a clerical collar, a stole, a couple of pairs of jeans, and some books; and set off. At the last minute, I went back up to my attic bedroom, put on the bracelet my friend Judy from the homeless community had given me, and tucked into my pocket the miniature plastic figurines of the Holy Family another dear friend from the community, Dave, had bought for me from the Catholic religious supply store down the road from the cathedral basement in which we'd gathered for more than a decade. "Your own family of *refuges*, sis," he'd said, transferring them from his shaking hand to mine. "Take them with you for protection."

I'd wrapped that bracelet round my wrist and carried those figurines in my pocket every morning since I'd been on the border, setting out with them as I walked from whichever hostel or Airbnb room I was staying in toward the places asylum seekers most typically gathered. I volunteered with legal clinics and health clinics and found ways to sit with and listen to, and do my best to actually hear the words of those with nothing left but their own strength and fierce determination and muted, heavy hope for a better life in the States.

Most days, the only thing I could think of to do after that was pray a few words of repentance handed down to us by the church. As I walked back out of the turmoil to the hushed safety of wherever I was staying, I'd fill my heart with the words, breathing them in and then out again, offering them up as I walked, step after step after step:

> Lord have mercy.
> Christ have mercy.
> Lord have mercy.

2

MORE DISPLACED MEXICANS arrived on the street next to the Paso del Norte bridge in downtown Juárez every day that first week. Almost all came from the three Mexican states most in thrall to the violence and corruption drug money brings in its wake: Zacatecas, Guerrero, and Michoacán. Narco-sponsored violence had been growing for years in Mexico, and I knew that in these states in particular, reliable governance had largely given way to the kinds of violent regulation meted out by heavily armed drug cartels whose leadership was constantly changing and whose turf was regularly challenged not by the state so much as by other cartels. Newspapers were full of stories of urban gun battles in broad daylight and brutal killings designed to send a message and kidnappings and systematized cross-country human trafficking networks and statewide extortion rackets. The situation was dire, and it was only growing worse.

But as a whole, Mexico was also thriving in ways most nations could only dream about, and life was so much worse in so many countries to the south that it seemed impossible that so many Mexican citizens would be fleeing for their lives in this way. South Americans, sure. Central Americans, of course. Folks from Cuba and Haiti and even from countries in Africa, traveling up through Mexico in hope of securing asylum in the States: all this had been happening for years. But *Mexicans* flooding to the border to request asylum? It was both unexpected and hard to believe.

Yet there they were: a group of elderly couples and young parents with children and large extended families of fifteen or twenty and single men and people of every kind crowding onto the street all together, without shelter or food or provision of any type at all.

By the beginning of the second week, the street had been officially closed off to traffic, and both sides of the sidewalk had been transformed into a patchwork of individual, personalized living spaces. Some were marked by the limits of a blanket spread smooth or a flattened cardboard box, others used stuffed-solid plastic duffle bags to serve as walls, and a few had shade-providing awnings made with tarps or cheap plastic rain ponchos strung at an angle. No one away from the street knew much about what was going on, though the Catholic laywoman who'd started the tent for people returned from immigration detention centers in the States, Cristina Coronado, told me that the same thing was happening at the city's other ports of entry as well. Suddenly, it seemed, Mexican citizens seeking protection in the United States were everywhere.

I began to stop at the street on my way back from the tent every day, loaded down with the formula, diapers, and soft drinks that Cristina and her colleague Sigrid Gonzalez let me take from the tent. After Sigrid and I struggled with a couple of pretty chaotic attempts at distributing things fairly, a young mother named Cecilia, who was sleeping with her two kids by an oversized downspout about two-thirds of the way down the block, offered to house the supplies and distribute them as needed throughout the day. An elderly man who'd taken the space on the sidewalk next to hers had found her an only slightly broken plastic milk crate in which to store the supplies. And from then on, Cecilia spent hours each day pulling one, two, three damp sheets of diaper wipes from their tightly wrapped plastic bricks and then sliding them into individual baggies before zipping them closed. "We have to make sure there is enough for everybody," she said, firm, clear, and apparently calm. "We have to take care of the little ones."

Shocked by the sight of so many people—and particularly of so many children—camping out by the city's ports of entry to the States, local government agencies repeatedly offered them space in the shelters set up for immigrants. But the people were wary. There were official-looking forms to fill out in the shelters, they'd been told, and copies made of state-issued IDs, and they preferred to stay anonymous out on the street. There was no real way of knowing, they said, exactly who was connected to the people with semiautomatic guns and open-topped jeeps and no visible humanity left in them who'd been terrorizing the small towns and mountainous villages from which they were in flight. Plus, the shelters were all far away. And with no process regulating their access to the border and no limits on their freedom of movement within what was, after all, their own country, they refused to go.

Besides, they told themselves, and me, and anyone who came by the street and asked: They believed in God, and if God willed them to cross soon, they would cross soon. And if God willed them to wait, they would wait. And while it was true that the US officials at the checkpoint on the top of the bridge kept turning them away, they did occasionally relent and let a family in to officially ask for asylum. And who was to say when that might happen next?

Only one thing was sure, a fruit seller from Guerrero whose entire family had been threatened by a local cartel after he begged for more time to pay their "protection" fees told me: no one on that street was going to risk missing the next time—maybe in an hour, or later that night, or early the next day, or the day after that—when US officials finally opened their hearts and let them all in. "Primero Dios," he told me, wrapping things up. "First, God willing." And "Si, si, primero Dios," the small group of men around him replied, echoing their amen down the block.

Perhaps three hundred people had moved onto the street by then, and with no organized help of any kind at all, food was becoming a problem. Precooked meals from street vendors were affordable for a time but wouldn't be for long, and fires to cook on were out of the question. By the end of the second week, though, it was water that was by far the most urgent need.

Temperatures regularly reached 110 degrees in the sun, and there was no shade on the street besides that which the people themselves had started to create with small sheets of plastic or cloth and string. Too-heavy-to-lift flats of plastic bottles disappeared in seconds when Sigrid and I brought them over from the tent in the back of her car. But these were unsustainably expensive. For a couple of days, Sigrid filled huge garbage bags with reusable water bottles that she'd collected from generous folks in the Catholic parishes of El Paso, but we soon switched to five-gallon garrafones because it was the only way we could even almost provide what was needed.

At first we brought two of the huge blue plastic water jugs to the street, setting them up on a miniature, folding pine table, with reusable spouts attached for pouring. A day later, the population had doubled, and we left four. Within a week, we were stacking up ten. Each day, a small group of men from the camp led me to a store about a dozen blocks away, which refilled each one for sixteen pesos—about eighty cents—from a coin-operated spigot in the wall. The plastic jugs were bulky and incredibly heavy when they were full. Empty, though, they were lighter than air. Young boys from the community, bored and eager to prove themselves, swung them onto their shoulders as we got ready to leave, only to be nudged aside by their fathers. "This one thinks he is a man already!" someone named Marco-Antonio said, and the others all laughed. Seeing his shame, the boy's father added, more fact than indulgence, "Soon, son, soon . . . but not yet."

On the way back to the street, when the garrafones were once again full, this same man stopped, turned suddenly to face me, and said, as if in response to a challenge I'd never made, "You know why I brought my family here?" There was only the faintest hint of a question mark at the end of this sentence, and I knew enough by then to say nothing at all in response to a question like that. We looked at each other for a moment, the man just a little bit crooked from the weight of the garrafón on his left shoulder. Then he snatched his eyes away, focused again on his feet, and continued: "They broke into the house, pushed us to the ground, snatched my two-year-old out of my wife's arms, and then put an AK-47 against his head. 'We will kill him if you don't pay,' they said. I begged them to please leave him alone—to put the boy down and kill me instead. But they laughed and said, 'No. You we will leave alive. It is him we will kill.'"

I'd heard many stories like this and not yet enough to numb me to them. A couple of months earlier in Tijuana, for example, I'd met a woman from Cameroon who'd arrived by bus from Mexico City, which she reached by plane from Nigeria, which she reached by walking for weeks through "the bush" in Cameroon. Her name was Yanelle, and she'd been stuck at the border for more than two months by the time I met her, sitting by herself in a brilliant green dress on the curb across the street from the tree under which Tijuana's sole border official sat doing his work.

I had run out of the informational fliers I was supposed to be distributing and had sat down next to her in the shade. For a time we sat quietly, watching the goings-on: the pushing to get to the gray plastic table under the tree, the back and forth with the official, the inevitable deflation of the petitioner, the retreat. After a while, she began to speak. I still don't know why this happened, but I'm grateful that it did. One minute she was sitting on the yellow painted curb, seemingly settled into the endless nothing of waiting, the next she'd turned to me and told me she'd left her daughter with her mother when she fled Cameroon.

"With my own mother," she repeated, leaning in, making sure I understood that she would have left her daughter with no one else. She herself had to flee, she added then, straightening her back and turning once more to stare straight ahead. She had to flee, she said again, and so she did.

I did my best to settle as we sat still and silent there on the curb, together and also not, I knew, watching the crowds on the other side of the street as they, too, waited and waited and waited. Then she started to speak again.

Three months after she left, soldiers "came to our village, shooting," she said. "Shooting and shooting." Everyone ran, and "when you are running like that, you do not know even if your own children are with you." Her mother had run with everyone else. When she stopped, she realized her granddaughter wasn't with her. She'd tried to run back to the village to find her, but the people she was with had stopped her; she would only die that way.

From that time to now, Yanelle said, still staring straight ahead, still matter of fact, "My daughter has not been heard from at all. She is fourteen, and I do not know how she will survive." She believed her mother was living "in the bush," though her cell phone no longer received calls. Yanelle had last spoken with her two months earlier, and she had no idea, that morning, where either her mother or her daughter was.

"For a mother, not knowing where your child is—that is the worst," she said. "If I could only hear that they are together, everything would be fine. But this . . ." She trailed off into silence, and for a time I followed her there—at least part of the way.

I also have children, two American young men, and these stories of violence against other people's kids always made me look away, both grateful for and ashamed of their own relative safety. Please, God, keep them all safe; please, God, keep these evils away, I'd pray, not daring to specify but wanting to.

3

COMBINED, EL PASO and Ciudad Juárez form the largest city on the US-Mexico border. Close to three million people live in the dusty, low-slung urban valley. Every day, tens of thousands of people cross between the two countries legally and in both directions: for school, work, shopping, medical appointments, visits with family, even a quick drink in a favorite bar. For all this, though, the two cities are extraordinarily different, and while El Paso is one of the safest cities in the United States, Juárez has long been one of the world's most dangerous.

Numbers are a lousy way to express an incarnate reality, I know. But just by way of shorthand for now, an average of four people were murdered in Juárez every day the year I was there.

During 2010, the city's worst year, when the army was brought in to quell the ravages of a turf war between two cartels, more than 3,500 people were killed. Things had improved a little since then. But still, in 2019, 1,499 people were murdered, and just the weekend before the Mexican asylum seekers arrived on the street, 23 people had been shot dead. Juárez was, in other words, a pretty rough place. Even people who loved it said as much.

Across the border, of course, was Texas: beige, low-slung, with huge skies, big trucks, ads for guns everywhere you turned, and giant, well-lit posters by the side of the highway that said things like:

Beyond Reasonable Doubt JESUS
Is Alive!
Call (83) FOR-TRUTH

A city full of violence on one side, then, and—for a half-English, half-Cuban, female Episcopal priest like me, at least—a city full of strangers, with strange ways, on the other.

I'd traveled to Juárez from Tijuana for what I thought would be a short visit, and I'd spent most of the first month believing I'd return to Tijuana, where I hoped to set up an open and multilingual space for prayer and companionship by the wall and the tree where asylum seekers gathered each morning before dawn. Pressed up against the Pacific, Tijuana has a coastal flavor I almost recognized. The air is moist, people's postures are loose, and right up alongside the suffering and the fear there is a kind of kitschy, seaside extravagance, which made it all seem almost tolerable.

On the corner outside the room I stayed in while I was there, for example, a man had painted two donkeys with black-and-white stripes so that they looked like zebras. And most every morning, on my way back from the wall, I passed families of tourists from the south arranged stiffly around them, grinning with delight or else somber in their gathered formality as they prepared for a photo.

Of course, the US-built wall that had come to define the border was inescapable there too. Eighteen feet tall, it curved through the city like a slinking dragon: up a hill here, down a hill there, cutting off streets and slicing through neighborhoods all the way to the beach and the sea. It would cut straight across the water, too, if we could figure out how, I'm sure. But for now, it stopped, headless and freed from purpose suddenly, thirty or forty feet out, where the heavy, gray waves of the Pacific pounding the wall's edges were lethal, too often, to those who tried to swim around.

Seven hundred miles inland and surrounded by desert, everything was different in El Paso–Juárez—everything except for the wall. Here, too, people tried to climb over it, often breaking their backs when they fell. And here, too, people drowned, not in the ocean but in the no less lethal waters of the Rio Grande. But I felt miles and miles from anything I knew, and it was only when the Mexican asylum seekers arrived that I started to think I would stay. Every day I spent a little more time in their camp on the street, and every day I got to know a little more deeply the men, women, and children who were trying to survive there, until, against my desire and despite my emerging plans, it started to feel that this was where I was supposed to remain.

I had rented a small room in a family's home in El Paso up close to the border by then. In part because it felt too peaceable and domestic—and also too lonely—sitting on the bed in my room as the family romped and rollicked its way toward supper each evening, I took to heading up into the mountains at the end of each day to sit and think and at least try to pray things through.

I wanted to leave; that's really all I knew—to go back if not to Boston, then at least to Tijuana. I was used to suffering and even, in far smaller doses, to horror. Twelve years of working with homeless people had taught me something about trauma, the ravages of chronic poverty, and the deep, surreal horror of becoming less and less visible even as you spend more and more of your day out on the street in full view. Praying and working and cooking and meditating and walking and writing and, most of all, loving and being loved by people like these had made me the priest that I was. My comfort with chaos—which is to say, with the unpredictable and ever-changing flux of life lived with very little agency or power to control—was part of what allowed me to believe that I'd be able to meet and be met by the people on the border and, with them, to catalyze at least some kind of supportive community that might help.

But the absence of anything in the least bit familiar in Juárez, and the landscape—which was beautiful, certainly, but also harsh and gray and without grass or trees or anything moist—and, most of all, the level of danger that was not localized now but everywhere: well, it frightened me. Wherever I turned I was confronted by symptoms of violence remembered, or of violence feared, or of violence about to happen. Layered, varied, and sometimes luridly visible, the pervasiveness of this violence was growing more and more apparent with each passing day, and I worried that I was starting to get lost in it.

Part of the trouble, I realized, was that I was a priest without a church, without a community, and without support, and the absence of all this had begun to feel critical. I hadn't understood this back in Boston, though people kept asking. "Who is sending you?" they'd ask. "It is important to be *sent*." And though I had the willing permission of my bishop, the only true answer I could ever give was, "Well . . . no one," because what bishop or diocese or church agency would send me to a place I couldn't yet name, to a work I couldn't yet imagine, with a people I hadn't yet met?

All I thought I knew was that the kind of work I'd learned how to do with folks back in Boston—people-centered, community-based work, not set apart from horror but lodged in its heart—could provide a real backstop against the splintering of suffering. And, again, before I could even begin to do work like this, I needed, simply, to be there: to meet and then listen and learn and see and feel at least some of the truths of the people who were right then bearing the weight of our immigration policies in their bodies. Which is what I was doing now, of course, volunteering with Cristina and with Sigrid in the big white tent and spending time with the people on the street leading to the bridge, doing very little that seemed useful even if you squinted at it.

But there was still so much I didn't know. Almost everything! Though physically a borderland myself, I did not understand the culture of the place. And my Spanish remained partial and wonky and so grammatically incorrect that even putting the words *grammar* and *my Spanish* together in a sentence felt like a lie. Many mornings I woke up, and many evenings I went to bed, too, convinced that I'd made a mistake and needed, simply, to leave.

But then I'd walk back across the bridge to the tent or the street in Juárez and be swept up again by the ocean of suffering and the reality of the violence and the danger that was everywhere and realize that none of these questions mattered very much in the end. Besides, it was becoming clearer to me each day that the church needed to be present to all this in an incarnate and practical way. Also, that far from being entirely *un*-up to the task, my work with homeless folks in Boston made me quite well suited to it. But it was dangerous in a different way in Juárez. And I had no place at all to both sink and be caught, and without that—without a community through whom I could reliably locate love and rest and peace—I worried I would fall apart.

By the beginning of the asylum seekers' third week on the street, though, the signs that I should stay were becoming indisputable. Honestly, I could practically see them as I settled into my spot high up on the mountain and tried to pray. I didn't want to stay, but this seemed to be where I was needed. I didn't want to stay, but this was why I came. I didn't want to stay, but I had to. A storm kicked up in the cavity of my chest then, a terrible thrashing, back and forth, back and forth, until it felt as if the movement itself between yes/no, yes/no, yes/no was in and of itself scouring and cleaning out and enlarging my heart. If this was discernment, I remember thinking, it was discernment as tumble dryer on high speed and high heat, thumping violently away inside as I sat, to all intents and purposes, as quiet and still as could be.

Looking out across the great sprawl of Juárez–El Paso, so clearly one city, dusty and dimly lit in the valley below, I tried to calm myself by focusing in. There was the Wells Fargo building, symbol of our country's preferential option for the rich and powerful, lit up fittingly that night in red, white, and blue. There, the terrible wall. There, the place where the train tracks crossed it, and the hideous red X sculpture in Juárez.

Allowing my gaze to glide across the valley in this way, lighting first on specific landmarks, then drifting down the molten stream of taillight-lit highway that meandered through it, I finally reached the valley's edge and the mountains that ringed it, dark and still. And there I saw for the very first time, tiny, barely more than a speck, but clear now, too, indisputable, at the top of the peak farthest off to my right: a silhouetted statue of Jesus, arms outstretched, cruciform. Cristo Rey. Christ the King.

Oh my God. Not to stay would be to run away. This is what I knew, all of a sudden: not to stay now would be to run away from him. And tell me, please, what in the world would there be to do after running away from Jesus?

I closed my eyes then and for a second felt as alone as I'd ever been in my life. Then a young couple, clearly there for the privacy as much as for the view, stumbled giggling onto my rock, arm in arm, apologized for getting in the way, and then stumbled away again, laughing some more. I started laughing myself then, just a little. Life was life was life wherever I was, I thought. And love was love was love. Brushing the dust off the seat of my jeans as I stood, I made a tiny little bow to Jesus on the horizon and the young couple and the dimly lit valley below, and I then turned and walked back to the road, filled with gratitude all of a sudden for the work that was, for a time, mine to do.

4

NEW GROUPS OF frightened and beleaguered families from Zacatecas, Guerrero, and Michoacán arrived on the street by the bridge every day those first weeks of September. Crossing Juárez Avenue weighed down by children too young to walk, bouquets of bulging plastic bags tied together with string, and too heavy suitcases hauled behind them like boulders, they made their way to the chiclet stand where the street began. Or they walked to the skinny overhang of the currency exchange store across from it and then stopped, literally stunned by what they saw: stretching down the street, all the way to the bus stop where the road curved, cutting off the rest from view, both sidewalks were entirely obscured by shade-giving shelters, constructed with blankets and tarps and spread-eagled jackets attached to poles and electrical wires with string. Under these structures women worked, keeping house, while along the street in between children played, and men gathered in pairs, or stood alone, making call after call after call to whoever they knew who had even a chance of offering some help.

There was, as yet, no organized or sustaining aid of any kind. But local people had started dropping by with what they had: large iceboxes on wheels, full of bean burritos, each individually wrapped in foil; baby clothes; a shopping bag full of Crayolas with sheets of photocopied coloring pages; a hobby horse; miniature cuddly toys with oversized eyes stretched wide;

T-shirts; sodas; little piles of cash. And with these the people made do. Between finding food, and caring for the children, and creating little temporary homes for their families on the sidewalk, the women gathered, stored, and then shared donations with as much generosity as possible. They directed newly arrived families to spots farther and farther down the block, past the bus stop and the defunct charging station, helping them settle in by offering a blanket if there was one or some food.

Abuzz with the frantic, suspended activity of in-between places everywhere, the community was energized also by fear. People had not simply traveled to this place, after all; they had fled there. While both dignity and trepidation kept most people's stories unspoken, newcomers sometimes believed that all they had to do was tell their story to an American to gain access to the States, and—as the only US citizen around most of the time—I was often the one they told them to.

In this way a man who'd claimed a spot on the corner closest to the bridge, a grandfather and patriarch of his family of ten from Michoacán named Martín, walked right up to me, as his wife did what she could to settle in, and said, flatly, "They shot me three times in the belly." When he lifted his shirt to show me, right there in the middle of the street, I forced myself to look and to at least try to let myself see: two rounded mounds; one long, roughly stitched slash.

He hadn't finished, though. "They cut off three fingers too. Look," he said, holding up a hand. "And slashed a machete through my skull," he added, removing his baseball cap to reveal a scar running from the top of his forehead, across the bald dome of his head, and all the way down to the thin ring of hair he had left at the back.

"They left me for dead," Martín said then. "But I'm harder to kill than that." And then again, he said, iced-over rage like cataracts in his eyes, "They thought they'd killed me, the narcos. But no."

It had been harder than anyone had expected to ask for asylum at the top of the bridge, even with stories like these. US Border Patrol had constructed a checkpoint right at the bridge's apex, where a thin, brass line marked the place Mexico stopped and the United States began. They'd done this, I'd learned, in order to prevent asylum seekers from stepping onto US soil. Requests for asylum from within the country had to be processed immediately. By keeping asylum seekers on the other side of the border, then, even by a couple of inches, officials were able to evade asylum laws and keep people out with the line they'd given Gabriela, and Yanelle, and most every asylum seeker at most every port of entry up and down the border: we have no room.

This was why Gabriela, her two kids, and her baby, Carlos, were still on the street two weeks after they arrived. And it was why the community was continuing to grow. No one kept records at first, but by the end of the first week, Luis Miguel had started keeping a tally, so we all knew that on days six, seven, and eight, no one had been allowed across the checkpoint to request asylum at all; that on day nine, two families had been allowed in; and then no one at all again on days ten, eleven, twelve, and thirteen.

On day fourteen, however, there was optimism. I arrived after a long morning in the tent, during which another volunteer and I had removed eighty-seven immigration detention center bracelets from children's wrists carefully, carefully, with scissors. A new team of officers had cycled onto the checkpoint, Martín told me almost the moment I arrived on the street, and they seemed kind, even concerned, and had promised to do what they could to get people through. They would know more at six o'clock, the official had said. And just like that, the hunched-over wiltedness of the days before plumped upright again. There was hope. There was the possibility of looking forward. There was, just around the corner, the next step on the journey that had otherwise been unrelenting.

Partly to celebrate and partly because I'd grown worried about rats, I decided to clean up the street a bit as we waited for news. Cristina had let me have some garbage bags and a broom from the tent, along with a box of blue latex gloves, and when I pulled the gloves out of my backpack on the street, Cecilia's little boy, five-year-old Tomás, asked to try on a pair. But his mother said, "No, no, they are not for playing," and I let it go. As I unfolded the garbage bag, though, I discovered that a long strip of bright yellow plastic was attached to it, like the tail of a kite. Seeing this, Tomás lit up again. He reached for it and held on, and in this way we set off down the street, he proudly marching ahead holding the yellow kite tail, leading the way, me behind him, picking up garbage.

Pretty soon an older kid from across the street asked if he could help, too, and I said, "Yes! But if you are really going to help, you will need to wear gloves." And we looked wonderful, the three of us, parading down the street with our blue gloves and our yellow kite tail, picking up garbage to a chorus of smiling thank-yous.

"We are a good team," I said as I thanked the boys after. But they didn't do it for the thanks; they did it for the blue gloves, which we took off when we were done and marveled at the sweat that made our hands look as if we'd just gotten out of the shower. The older boy, José Luis, asked if we could do all this again tomorrow, and when I said yes, he nodded like a man and then showed me he could tie a knot in the almost-full black garbage bag by himself. Then he and Tomás hauled it across the street to the place the community had designated for garbage, and I went to join the adults, who were gathering down the other end of the street, by the bridge.

It was almost six, time to send someone up to the checkpoint, and when one of the water carriers, Humberto, volunteered, everyone agreed he would do. Up he went, alone in his red shirt, and you could see the solid-wallness of his back muscles under the red as he walked. The rest of us stood clustered together by the chiclet stand on the corner, watching and waiting, and I have never strained my eyes so much to see what I could not possibly see as we stood there, and stood there, and stood there. Then, finally, Humberto came back, less solid than he had been, deflated.

"Not yet," he said, shaking his head. "They said to try back an hour from now. . ."

This happened over and over again. Twice that third week alone. "Perhaps half, perhaps more than half, of the families will be allowed through at nine," an officer at the top of the bridge told a man named Nicolás on the sixteenth day. "We're working on it and will let you know." But then nine came, and one of the leaders who had emerged in the community—Ángel, in this case—paid his three pesos and walked up to the top of the bridge, where Border Patrol told him, "Not yet. Come back at ten." So another leader went back at ten, when they were told, "Come back at three" when they were told, "Not today."

And between all this, the rumors. Arriving on the street from the tent around two on the nineteenth afternoon, for example, I found the entire community—almost three hundred people by then—standing in a neat, straight line, kids with their backpacks strapped tight against their backs, parents with great bundles under their arms, waiting in the searing sun. And then, perhaps forty-five minutes later, I watched as the line dissolved. Two days after that, word had again spread that they would all be allowed in, and everyone had packed up everything but the shells of houses they'd constructed with tarps and garbage bags and cardboard. Then they sat exposed on the curb, still and silent and keeping their children close, waiting for the moment when they would be called. But they were never called.

To this the people said, We must have patience. We must wait. We must remain organized and peaceful and quiet.

"Primero Dios," Humberto summed up, as always. And it was a huge grace, this faith—it must have been. But the order and the patience and the ability to endure—historic, you could feel it, formed through centuries—didn't seem to be getting them anywhere. I felt my American-ness more and more each day.

It wanted to scream.

I wanted to scream.

5

THE STRAINING OF asylum seekers through the mostly clogged sieve of the checkpoint at the top of the bridge has a name. It is called *metering*. And, like so many policies that rule the lives of tens of thousands of people stuck up and down the southern side of the border, it is illegal.

It is important to be clear here: everyone on the street was seeking asylum in the States, which is to say that everyone was seeking the legal and physical protection of a neighboring country in the face of ongoing and lethal threat at home. This right was established in 1951, when the United States joined 148 other countries in signing the United Nations' Refugee Convention, which was later ratified again—and also expanded—in 1967.

Asylum seekers are not trying to sneak into the country, in other words, but to enter it legally. Except there was not much left of the US asylum process anymore. For years it had been more complex than it should have been, and by 2019, it had become as baroque and Kafkaesque as an absurdist play. Honestly, the truest thing to say is that after decades of neglect and three years of concerted administrative and political undermining, there was really no effective asylum system left, nothing that resembled a predictable or ordered process at all.

What there was instead—really *all* there was instead—was metering, which never overtly denied the right of those in flight from their own country to request the immediate protection of another but which did manage to stall the process so effectively that it became pretty much the same thing.

Most basically, then, metering meant that officers never said no to a request for asylum. Saying *no* would be flatly illegal, and in all my time on the border, I never once heard anyone say it. What they said instead is "Not right now." Or "We have no room." Or "We are full." Or "Try back later." Or even, occasionally, "We wish we could let you in, but sadly we are full right now."

Because "we are full," people seeking the protection of the United States are not, strictly speaking, denied access to the asylum process. They are simply being told that they must wait. There is a backlog, officers explain, sometimes apologetically and sometimes not, so instead of being given the opportunity to lodge their request with an asylum officer, they need to take a number on the waiting list: 3,967, for example, or 4,581, or 5,190. Some days, but not all—and no one knows when or why this is so—a few of these numbers are called. Sometimes just one. Sometimes five. Sometimes none. There is no predictability to the way this process unfolds. No reliable pattern whatsoever. The only certain thing is that more numbers are given out than are called each day and that as a result, the number of people in flight for their lives who are stuck in cities up and down the southern side of the border continues to grow.

US officials insist these lists are created by Mexican authorities and have nothing to do with their own, more official regulation of the border. But everyone knows they are both created and maintained on behalf—and at the behest—of the United States. Far too unreliable and open to manipulation to deserve the status it is granted, this list is the one to which every non-Mexican asylum seeker at the border must add their name. There was never any certainty about how long it might take to get from the bottom of it to the top, but it typically took somewhere between five months and a year.

Most asylum seekers from Central and South America travel for months just to get to the border between Mexico and the United States. These are dangerous, often brutally hard journeys that regularly inflict as much harm as the harm asylum seekers originally fled from. Some are robbed, others kidnapped and then held for ransom, and still others are murdered. The most appalling case dates back to 2014, when a grave containing the remains of 198 Central American migrants was found near the US border in Tamaulipas. Local police worked as lookouts for the cartel that did the killing that day, which was part of the reason the case drew so much attention. Since then the kidnappings have only grown more sophisticated. Dead migrants don't turn a profit, after all, while kidnapped living ones often bring in a fortune in ransom money.

There are pages and pages of horrifying statistics about the dangers of this journey, but, for now, here is just one: 80 percent of female migrants traveling through Mexico to the border are sexually assaulted on their way.

Eighty percent.

By the time they arrived in places like Juárez, then, mothers and children and grandfathers and aunts from some of the most violent and ravaged countries across the globe were wrung out, desperate, and violently traumatized. Most often, their money had run out or been stolen, and their temporary, pass-through

Mexican visas had too. No matter where they were from, or what they had suffered, or who they had violently lost to brutality so gory it was impossible to fully imagine—husbands' bodies shredded in machines meant for agriculture, wives raped and then beaten to death, children executed by a single gunshot to the head—they now had to stop, take a number, and wait. Unless they had money. If they had money, there was a good chance they could bribe their way up close to the top of the list. But if they didn't—and most didn't—well, they could only try to figure out how to survive while they waited for who knew how many months in any one of the strange border cities that kill so many of their own.

Only Mexican citizens were exempt from the intentional, extended delay of metering through what was known to everyone simply as "la lista." As citizens of the country from which they were right then seeking to flee, their need for protection had an urgency few others could reasonably claim. Even a minimal delay at the border kept them trapped in the country they claimed was persecuting them, and because of this the United States hadn't yet come up with a way to delay their request for asylum.

Once, a station chief at a local port of entry insisted that Mexicans could never be subjected to metering of any kind at all. But that was later. At the beginning, all we knew was that being Mexican made not a shred of difference at the checkpoint and that Border Patrol officers routinely used the same delay tactic with Mexican citizens as they did with everyone else, sending them back down the bridge to the street because they were "full," day after day after day, even as the same dangers waited for them there as waited for asylum seekers from every other country on earth.

And if all this wasn't enough, human traffickers and coyotes and narco foot soldiers and scam artists of all kinds prowled through the places both international and Mexican asylum seekers gathered. They offered quick crossings with small, hidden bundles, or quick money for sex, or at least relief if you'll just smoke some of this or shoot up some of that. So, scattered through the places where mothers stood with young children weighed down by suitcases and single men tried to shrink themselves into nothingness, there were people who had lost hope and so lost themselves. One afternoon on the street that first month, I did what I could to prevent a group of wide-eyed kids from staring too long at such a man, a Central American migrant who was sitting in the middle of Juárez Avenue, arms stretched above his head with two bleeding wrists, toilet paper bandages unraveling down from them, each square splotched with their own bloody pattern.

He wasn't harming anyone, the man. He was just sitting there, straight-legged as a toddler, squirting window-washing fluid onto his head and then rubbing with his hands as if it were shampoo. Only it wasn't shampoo, and it didn't make a lather, so he kept squirting more and more toxic cleaner onto himself and then rubbing harder and harder until the blood-splotched toilet paper started to tear.

And in the face of this man's real and terrible pain, what did I do? Well, once I got the kids away, I walked right on past him, as I walked past so many, speechless and stunned and afraid.

6

FOR A TIME, authorities hoped the influx of asylum seekers from Michoacán, Zacatecas, and Guerrero was just a blip, a random wave of migration that would recede as suddenly as it had surged with little explanation and no need for action. But this wasn't turning out to be the case. Families continued to arrive each day, sometimes by the hundreds, sometimes just a handful, and numbers were growing at three of the city's four ports of entry.

At the end of the third week, Cristina and Sigrid invited me to an emergency meeting at which federal, state, and city politicians, the International Red Cross, and academics and representatives of NGOs from both sides of the border gathered. Crowded around a huge square table in suits and robust-looking work uniforms and official-looking bibs emblazoned with primary-colored insignia, they looked impressive and ready to get things done.

I sat against the wall with other extraneous types, astonished and impressed by the display. For a time it was all action. People greeted each other like long-lost friends, and as the room filled, so the energy increased. When the mic was turned on, though, and the meeting officially began, every department head, and government official, and NGO representative delivered their own version of the same speech: about their long-standing work along the border, their future dreams, and their plans to resolve the hemisphere-wide migration crisis. As minutes turned to hours, the energy in the room began to dwindle.

Soon enough, people started to drift out through the glass doors, into the corridor, with cell phones. A few slipped into the elevator and never came back, until, a couple of hours in, I saw a small group of folks in jeans and sneakers beginning to huddle in the corner. Chowing down churros and knocking back coffee, they spoke quietly and quickly to each other as if in shorthand, scrawled notes on scraps of paper, asked practical questions, made simple suggestions, nodded, and generally got done what needed to be done.

Cristina Coronado was one of these people. Approaching fifty and dressed in sneakers, a pair of old jeans, and a ragged black T-shirt, she worked with a small group of Roman Catholic missionaries, the Columbans, who cared about how migrants were being treated in their city and who had put that caring into action step by step, practical detail by practical detail, for years. It was Cristina who, with Sigrid, led the work in the big white tent in which all returnees from the States were now welcomed, and it was she who had pressured Roman Catholic bishops and governmental department heads and academics and volunteers of all kinds to support and sustain it. It was also she to whom hundreds of individual asylum seekers turned, calling one of her multiple cell phones day and night, asking for advice, asking for connections, asking for emergency interventions, all of which she did what she could to provide through her hugely diverse network of connections across the city.

Utterly determined to see things through, Cristina had the kind of ribald, swingy presence that came from working, always, close to the people on the ground and so knowing the situation better than anyone. This clearly rankled the more professional types. But the authority of her work was real nonetheless, unassailable. And in the end, it was she who closed the meeting.

"Thank you—truly, thank you all for being here today," she said, her younger, more polished colleague Sigrid translating into English, sentence by sentence. "We've heard so many wonderful ideas, and lofty plans, and beautiful dreams." Here she paused to look around the table, smiling, her teenage-style braces flashing incongruously. "Perhaps—by God's grace—we will achieve them all one day. In the meantime, though," she continued, looking straight ahead now, her smile replaced by the anguished and urgent expression I'd seen on her face every day, "we are facing the reality of hundreds of families living out on the streets of our city without food or shelter or medical care. . . . Let's let that reality be our teacher for now, no?"

Limited emergency assistance kicked in on the street the very next day. In addition to the food she'd been collecting for the tent from Catholic parishes in El Paso, where she lived, Sigrid set up a donation center in her parents' Mexican restaurant there, organizing teams to make five hundred additional packed lunches every morning for the people on the street. Just a couple of days after the meeting, Cristina also managed to galvanize the Mexican Marines into cooking one hot meal a day out of a mobile kitchen parked in the lot of the city's largest migrant shelter.

The first day this happened, I went with her to pick up the food, and it was mind-blowing to see the size of the vats they were cooking with. They were of a size I'd previously only imagined from fairy tales, easily big enough to cook children in. Each one held enough food to feed four hundred people.

In order to maintain at least a little separation between the Mexican government and the Mexican asylum seekers, the food was not distributed by the marines but by representatives from the International Red Cross, with help from Sigrid and three or four random others like me. For some reason, the Red Cross workers dressed in starched, white uniforms like nurses from an old-fashioned war. They arrived on the street in a large white van every day around three, and most days I helped them set up, and then serve, before continuing on with them to the communities at the other two bridges. It was so hot in the sun that a man named Oscar made parasols for us from pieces of cardboard speared through by splintery shards of plank he'd scavenged from empty lots in the neighborhood. The days were full of moments of surreal grace like this, and I was growing more and more reluctant to leave the people gathered at the foot of the Paso del Norte to go with the Red Cross and with Sigrid to the communities of asylum seekers at the next bridge, and then the next.

Nothing was more important than the basic distribution of food, obviously. But I've never been good at handing out bowl after bowl after bowl after bowl. I'd get distracted—and the line would clog—as I kept being drawn to meet people. I mean really meet, without the food between us. It was the same in the big white tent too. Day after day I did the minuscule things I could there—tying new shoelaces into kids' tiny sneakers, and handing out sandwiches, and offering toothpaste and T-shirts and fresh pairs of socks—until I remembered how even two hours of distributing things like this separated those who were there to give from those who needed help in ways that were both disturbing and unreal. Standing behind tables laden with necessities, volunteers became—within hours!—the people who had everything, even as asylum seekers became the people who had nothing. And within a couple of days, their need started to seem unpleasant and taxing—rude, even.

People never talk about this because it's shameful, I guess. But the truth is that it happens to volunteers in places of struggle and pain all the time. In the tent one morning just a few days before Oscar gave me my first splintery parasol, for example, a single mother with three children under seven, just released from detention after months of trying to survive in Juárez, and longer than that away from her home on a coffee plantation in the mountains of Guatemala, approached the table at the back of the tent. There she asked quietly, and with visible embarrassment, for a pair of shoes. In response, a young volunteer, an undergrad studying art history in El Paso, was able to tell her with equanimity, "I'm sorry. We have none"—when she knew there was a giant cardboard box of shoes just next door. But this volunteer had been working in the tent for months by then, and she had grown so used to the suffering she saw there, day after day after day, that it had become, simply, part of the way things were. Besides, she told me later, she'd glanced to the ground, seen that the woman already had a pair of shoes, and decided they were good enough. "I can't believe she would expect new ones!" she said.

This is what I mean when I say that giving unilaterally day after day can never lead to healing for anyone. It was one of the first things homeless folks had taught me back in Boston, and it is what asylum seekers were teaching me now, all over again.

It is why, too, one afternoon about a week after the Red Cross started bringing hot food to the street, I asked Sigrid if I could stay with the people downtown instead of continuing on with her to the communities at two of the other bridges, Libre and Zaragoza. I needed to remain a little longer, I said, using that most essential word from the Gospel of John: to *remain* and be with the people there, even when I had nothing to give.

I'd see her the next day in the tent, I told her when she agreed. Waving goodbye, I watched as she pulled away in the minivan she had borrowed from her aunt, the giant vats now only half full of rice and beans still slopping onto the floor.

7

THIS WORK OF simply being with people had often gotten me in trouble as an Episcopal priest in the States. Our ministry in Boston rubbed many people in the church the wrong way: the liberals because we didn't haul those of us who slept on the street or in shelters up the hill to the State House and put placards in their hands in the name of "social justice;" the conservatives because they simply didn't seem to want to share our space, time, or treasure with such a ragged group of people, some of whom suffered from mental illness, others who drank, and still others who insisted on lugging their possessions around with them in bulging black garbage bags.

If the church was going to spend time with people experiencing homelessness, these factions seemed to agree, then we should at least focus our energies on doing stuff for them: providing, as efficiently as possible, what they seemed to so obviously need. Instead, we resisted the sometimes overwhelming urge to set about fixing things and spent our energies focusing on the people themselves, just exactly as they were, working with them to create a reliable and wide-open space for anyone and everyone who wanted, even fleetingly, to belong. And to belong not as guests in need—not even as honored guests in need—but as full-fledged, voting members of the community, whose real strengths and often long unseen gifts were first noticed and then required by the rest of us.

Real mutuality like this—the messy give and take of it, its necessary acceptance of all our needs and all our strengths—lay at the heart of everything we did back in Boston. It was hard to call the work political, but it was nothing whatsoever like charity. Instead we offered together an ongoing stream of relationship, possibility, and choice, through which street people were invited out of isolation and a sense of superfluity into the life-giving reality of being seen and known and needed.

The community that resulted was transformative, unpredictable, highly energized, deeply faithful, overflowing with love both given and received—and utterly lacking in anything like conventional piety. Sometimes gifts were offered, and received, with the kind of generosity that only the penniless have access to. Sometimes there were fights. And through it all we maintained our focus on the essential and beloved nature of every single person among us, insisting that, no matter what, each one of us was unique and each one of us was required for the growth of us all.

It drove people crazy.

In the Roman Catholic world, however, there is a well-established precedent for accompanying people in this way. Part of the reason I'd originally gone to Juárez was to meet a ninety-six-year-old former fighter pilot turned Catholic priest and his long-term coworker, an eighty-five-year-old Sister of Mercy who'd been living in the city for more than twenty-five years. Peter Hinde and Betty Campbell were living icons of the kind of Catholic activism that took root in Latin America in the latter half of the twentieth century. Radical, deeply dedicated, and unwaveringly aligned with those who were poor and powerless, they'd spent decades supporting impoverished rural communities with their presence, prayer, and, in Betty's case, medical care. Then they'd spent decades more fomenting change movements in Washington, DC, through a Catholic Worker house they founded named Tabor House. An old friend of mine in Boston had worked with Peter and Betty in El Salvador, and I'd spent hours communicating with Betty over email since he introduced us. But nothing could have prepared me for the power of who she was—and is.

Betty came to meet me by the giant pink cross at the foot of the bridge the first time I met her. In her worn, sensible shoes, long-sleeved shirt, sagging gray slacks, and with her long white hair piled up on her head, she looked exactly like Dorothy Day, only bursting with laughter and light. We took two buses to get from the bridge to their simple home with a rickety wooden fence and a mural of Mexico's patron saint, the Virgin of Guadalupe, on the front.

Inside, the central space was decorated with black-and-white photos and slightly faded portraits in pencil of their friends who'd been killed as a result of their work with impoverished communities, mostly in Latin America. They were all there: Sisters Maura Clarke, Ita Ford, Dorothy Kazel, and lay missionary Jean Donovan, who had been raped and then murdered in El Salvador in 1980, and two of the six Jesuit priests killed there nine years later, Frs. Ellacuría and Martin-Baró. When I commented on this, Betty stopped what she was doing and gazed at the images, beaming.

"Yes…" she said. "Aren't they wonderful? One time someone asked, 'Don't you find it depressing having all these photographs of dead people around you?'" she added, chuckling as she boiled water for tea. "And I said, 'Well, no. We don't think of them as dead. They are right here living with us—part of our family!'" I was smitten.

Peter came in and out that day, sprightly and handsome, while Betty made tea and set out a couple of plates and a single knife and a spoon on the table. She was a nurse as well as a nun and had been sent to Peru in the early 1960s to serve a small parish clinic just south of Cusco. Peter had arrived as a priest there a couple of years later, and for a time they worked closely together at the school and in the hospital and the parishes.

Things might have stayed that way forever, both of them working with others to improve the lives of poor people in ways long prescribed by the church, except one afternoon two Peruvians they sang with in the choir Betty had started asked to speak with them privately. They appreciated the help the church was bringing them, they said, but they hoped Peter and Betty might see, too, that no one from the local community had ever actually asked for the help and that, honestly, it would be better for everyone if religious communities like theirs would "stop moving, uninvited, into our home and then rearranging all of our furniture."

"As they spoke, we realized that everything they said was true," Betty told me, sitting at her kitchen table in Juárez now, nodding with an astonished kind of gratitude at the memory still, more than fifty years later. "No one in town ever asked us to build the big new school we had built. In fact, they already had a school! It was small. It was poor. But it was theirs. And we'd just ignored all that and done what the bishop wanted," she said.

"Which was to build a large school on the American model and to do the same with the clinics and the hospitals.

"It was a very important teaching for us," Betty told me then. "Very, very important. And from that time, we began to change the way we went about doing things. Accompaniment is what we try to live now. Accompaniment," she said again. "Living with others without trying to move their furniture around. It's why we moved here. We wanted to insert ourselves into life here quietly."

This is just exactly what Betty and Peter have done. For more than twenty years, they have lived simply in a neighborhood named Insurgentes—"Isn't that great?" Betty said, beaming—alongside everyone else. They facilitate support groups at their house, hold daily prayer services, advocate for all who ask, and welcome whoever comes into their home as if they were their long-lost brother or sister. Peter bakes two loaves of bread every week, and Betty harvests vegetables from a garden she has planted around a labyrinth made of pebbles. Every single Friday, for decades, the two of them catch a string of buses to get downtown and then walk across the bridge—and the border—to El Paso, where they lead a small peace protest in front of city hall. Betty sews enormous banners for this, which they roll up and carry with them in a rickety shopping cart. She makes protest posters along the back wall of their yard at home too. On one she has carefully written the names of each of the 263 journalists who had been killed in Mexico since 1993; on another, the names of the 56 priests killed there since 1990. A third poster lists the full names of the 43 students disappeared in Ayotzinapa in 2014, whose bodies have still not been found, and she is working on a list of the 1,970 women and the 18,443 men killed in Ciudad Juárez since 1993. She prays with these lists every day. And in this way they live, two poor and faithful people among the poor.

Life isn't easy. There isn't enough money sometimes, and the neighborhood is dangerous enough that when they leave the house, they do so separately in hopes of fooling would-be robbers into believing someone is still at home. But through it all, and most centrally, they seemed deeply and visibly happy, full of whatever the opposite of lonely is.

"There's one other thing," Betty said before I left, reaching across the table to hold my hand when Peter stepped out of the room. "I want you to know that we are *not* a couple. People often leave here thinking we are, but we are not.

"It has been a huge sacrifice," she said quietly then, "because of course I love him so much. But it is important to us both that we keep our vows."

Taken aback a little, and also hugely moved, I leaned toward Betty. "Can I ask you something personal that you don't have to answer?"

"Anything," she said.

"Are your vows the only reason you are not a couple?"

"Oh, yes!" she replied, clearly surprised by the thought that there could be another reason. "Only because of the vows!" she said and then threw her hands up in the air and laughed, and I just sat there astonished and still for a moment and then bent down to kiss the back of her hand because . . . well, what else was there to do?

Here is their unofficial rule of life—words they heard someone preach decades ago, typed up, wrapped in plastic, pinned to the wall, and then spent the rest of their lives trying to make manifest:

> *THE PERMANENT STRUGGLE TO CHANGE THE CONDITIONS OF LIFE FOR OUR PEOPLE CONSTITUTES:*
>
> *OUR PROFESSION OF LIFE,*
> *OUR SONG OF LOVE,*
> *THE CELEBRATION OF MEMORY,*
> *TAKING THE CHRISTS DOWN FROM THEIR CROSSES,*
> *GIVING OUR WHOLE HEART,*
> *SOWING DIGNITY,*
> *RISKING OUR VERY LIFE*
>
> *FOR THE POOR AND THOSE IN NEED*

Clearly, I had a lot to learn.

8

BY DAY TWENTY-NINE, the community had started to get organized. Teams had been formed to receive, store, and distribute the ad hoc donations of food, tents, blankets, mattresses, formula, and diapers for the babies. And, in response to complaints from officers at the top of the bridge, a small group of elected leaders drew up a list of families on the street, in their order of arrival, so they could begin to self-regulate access to the checkpoint.

Community-wide meetings had started, too, and every afternoon, hundreds of people gathered for them just past the international bus stop, halfway down the street. One of the leaders—a deportee from California who wore an eye patch like a pirate and whom everyone always and simply called Negrito—generally started these meetings off by standing on a wooden box and sharing announcements:

1. All parents *must* watch their own children!
2. No leaving the bridge bathroom wet underfoot, or the officials will be forced to shut it down again.
3. Do not let your children play with the water. Our water is for drinking, not playing!
4. Mothers can take only three diapers and one baggie of wipes at a time. We have to share. We need to make do.

People listened to these notices the way people everywhere listen to notices: sometimes carefully and sometimes not. The moment a younger leader—a fresh-faced cab driver from Michoacán named Hector—stood up and started reading from the community's newly compiled list, however, the crowd jostled in close and started paying attention. This was really why they gathered: for the roll call.

The community list now governed who went up to the checkpoint and when. The first family to arrive was placed at number one on the list, and they would go up to the checkpoint first; the second family to arrive was placed at number two, and they would go up next, and so it went, all the way down to family number seventy-four, who had just arrived. Hector read the last names of each family in order, and one by one, an adult representative of that family raised a hand, or a hat, or—if they were in the front—simply nodded. If you missed a day, your name was marked with a highlighter pen. If you missed two, you lost your place and were given a new number—at the bottom of the list.

I went to most of these meetings and tried my best to hang around at the edge of the crowd, keeping quiet, listening, learning, sometimes chatting with a mom or taking a couple of kids out of the huddle so their parents could focus. It was there that I met a broad-shouldered man with a prematurely lined face named Isaías.

He was reading as he stood in the community huddle, waiting for his name to be called. On a street packed with folks just trying to survive, it was rare to see someone standing around with a book, and when I asked what he was reading, he lifted it up to show me the cover: Narcotics Anonymous. For a time we stood next to each other in silence, listening as the names of heads of families were called off: Gabriel Alberto Reyna, Jesús José Lopez García, Luis Reynaldo Alvarez. When his own name was called, Isaías raised the book into the air, made eye contact with Hector, and then asked if I had a moment to talk.

Even before we got to the end of the street closest to the bridge, and to the relative privacy that the currency exchange alcove offered there, he started to tell me about his son. Twenty years old and killed, he said, just like that. And not killed only, tortured first. Isaías found out when he was called by "una oficina municipal," which told him they had a corpse he might be interested in.

Then they sent him the photos.

Here Isaías started to cry.

"First tortured and then shot," he said again, shaking his head minutely, willing the images gone. "Ach, but there are many ways to die," he added, gathering himself. "I myself am mostly dead these days."

He was carrying on as best he could, he said. Trying to find a way. But he was only half there, he knew, only half alive, and it was all he could do to keep it together for the son he still had with him. He cried again then, this working man with the broad shoulders and seemingly endless physical strength, this man not used to crying.

"I do not know if I have done the right thing coming here," he said. "But my younger son stopped leaving the house after the photographs came. 'Won't they kill me too?' he kept asking. 'I'll be next—they will kill me too!' And what could I say? Nothing, except pack what I could and get him out of the house." Here Isaías nearly cried again. "We had a house," he said.

"Who knows whether coming here was the right thing to do or the wrong thing to do? All I know is that I am doing my best to do as the book says," he said then, raising the small red book a fraction. "We can't do anything on our own, it tells me. We need the help of God—or of something like God. For me? I believe in God and in Jesus Christ, and I am simply trying to place myself in his hand," he said, and I was so moved by that singular: his hand.

"I am trying to place myself in his hand," he said again, "and carry on. With him, perhaps, there is a chance."

I thought Isaías would stop then, run out of words, sink into the kind of absence the inexpressible so often draws out. But the current of his words led him instead into another story, this time about his neighbor who was also taken, and then tortured, and then shot. This happened a lot on the street. Instead of leading to silence, a horror of this magnitude led most often to the telling of another horror, and then another, and another, the words multiplying instead of disappearing until emotions finally became blunted enough to go on.

"He made sacks," Isaías told me then. "I made pallets, and he made sacks, and we were friends all our lives. But one day—who knows why?—they took him. They asked for a ransom of a million pesos. Of course his wife didn't have a million pesos—who does? So they did what they do: they tortured him terribly and then shot him dead."

On nights I heard stories like that, I vegetated. I'd cut up some cheese, put it on a plate next to a premixed salad, and then take it into my little pink room and sort of cease.

I had moved, by then, to a small house at the foot of a cliff of gray dust. Heavily wrapped phone wires sagged over the narrow yard, along which hundreds of pigeons perched, packed tight, all the way across. My roommate was a young photographer just a couple of years older than my sons, and I was overwhelmed with gratitude that he didn't up and leave the minute he heard his new roommate was a middle-aged Episcopal priest. Still. Those first few weeks he was not entirely happy about the situation, and I'd been trying to clean the place in stages, when he was out, so he wouldn't get mad.

Some nights my roommate would come back with an oversized Styrofoam container of cheap Chinese food, and I was grateful to sit with him then and listen to his stories about the local newspaper scene. Other nights I'd try to woo the stray cat from the yard into the house, but she'd only ever accept food and never once let me touch her. I hardly ever dared call my kids. Partly this was guilt over their relative well-being, and partly it was superstition: if I kept them separate from all of this, perhaps they would stay safe.

There was so much suffering and so little action, that was the thing. And in the face of the immutable and implacable *no* of the border, my human need to do and do and do was being chastened and cut off at every turn, until the truth of my own puny presence—so small as to be almost absurd—became inescapable.

Desperate to do something, I called old friends in the press to let them know about what I'd begun to think of as a humanitarian crisis. But this was just the latest in a too long string of crises on the border, my US journalist friends reminded me, and no one was really interested.

"How many people are there?" the bureau chief of a national paper asked.

"Almost five hundred," I said.

"Terrible." He sighed, clearly moved. But I could tell from his tone that it wasn't enough. "Keep me posted, okay?" he said then. "And take care!"

No one else returned my calls at all.

The church, at least, was generous. I had official permission from the Episcopal Diocese of the Rio Grande to be there by then. But there was, as yet, no formal agreement about what exactly they would allow or encourage me to do. I'd been in regular contact with the bishop's right-hand man, Lee, and after coming to meet some of the asylum seekers on the street, he'd told me to buy what was needed and then send him receipts. Anything under $150 I could purchase without prior clearance, he told me, and straight after I went to a Walmart Superstore in Juárez and spent way more than that buying every single soft velour blanket they had in the store.

"Can you believe it? Brightly colored blankets for the kids: this is all I can do," I told a friend back in Boston on the phone. No wonder I felt so alone. Sitting endlessly on the sidewalk, in the heat that never ended, doing not much of anything but listening to stories of the horror so many others were experiencing was not easy. Who else could stand the frustration or the terror turned to boredom by this stupor of powerlessness?

I'd set up a little altar on top of the chest of drawers in my room by then: two images of Jesus, a brass cross with the prodigal son in the arms of the father at its heart, a candleholder with candle, a marble from the homeless community that looked like the earth, and a photo of each of my sons. That night, completely at a loss in the face of Isaías's pain, I lit the candle, then climbed onto the bed and sat with them all. I tried to be in silence, but that was impossible. So I sang bits of hymns I remembered instead, and then portions of chants, and then parts of the liturgy. I tried again to settle into silence, and then gave up again, and started to sing the Our Father, over and over, remembering Simone Weil, who had done the same, only silently in her head. She'd started the prayer again from the beginning every time her attention wandered. But my attention seemed cued only to wandering, so I tried reading a section from the Gospel of John and listening to a sermon posted online by one of the brothers in a monastery I spent a lot of time in back home.

And then I did it all again. And again. And again—until I was finally released into the present and the inevitable, liberating truth that it held: "I am useless, of course!" I understood again, as if for the very first time. "And I am powerless, of course! And I am finite and timid and unprepared, and I have no answers to give anyone at all, of course! But here I am, as they say. Here I am."

And for that day, at least, it felt like enough.

9

BY THE START of week five, kids had made a clear hierarchy of value for the latex gloves we used to collect the trash. It went, from bottom to top: Plain white. Thick white. Blue. Thick blue. White with powder. Blue with powder. Blue gloves with powder were almost impossible to find, and we hardly ever had them. Most often we were stuck with plain white or plain blue, which disappointed the kids, but they never complained.

More than twenty kids of all ages were gathering every day to clean the street by then, and all day long they came running up to me to ask: Is it now? Is it now? The gathering of trash had become a kind of liturgy—a real work of the people, which is what that word literally means. Every day we gathered at two, or as close to two as possible. Then the medium-sized kids distributed garbage bags to each team of three or four, while the bigger kids helped the littlest ones with their gloves. When everyone was ready, we spread out through the street like a diminutive army, asking each family in turn if they had anything they wanted to throw out.

Some kids made up chants for this process of requesting and receiving and thanking. "Any garbage?" they sang as they walked. "Any garbage today, señores? ¡Gracias, señor! ¡Gracias, señora!" And the parents—the moms mostly—beamed indulgently and then rummaged around their little structures until they found a bottle, or a wrapper, or an empty bag of chips still damp with lime, which they then handed over triumphantly to the kids—happy to make them happy in their attempts to do the same for them.

Afterward, the kids and I regrouped on the corner, compared bags for fullness, and told each other how incredibly well we had done ("Look, look, I even have a balloon!" one little girl exclaimed, plunging into the depths of her outsized black garbage bag and pulling it out in triumph). Then we'd strip off and throw out the gloves, teach each other how to tie knots, and finally take a photo of everyone's hands—which, on the best days, were coated in a fine layer of white powder.

We were gathering six or seven industrial-sized bags full of garbage each day, and it was good. But it was also still garbage collection, and I kept being snagged by the thorny idea that I really should be doing better than this, that in the absence of anything like school for the kids, there should at least be some kind of class.

I procrastinated for days, though. "Maybe tomorrow? Yes, tomorrow is much better—tomorrow for sure," I'd tell myself over and over. But in the end the classes simply had to start, so they did.

It's important to say here that I am in no way qualified to teach little kids anything. In my panic even at the thought of running a class, I spent more than $125 on packets of lesson plans and supplies from Amazon—the only usable part of which was a giant box of sidewalk chalk, which we went through in under a week.

God provided in the end, though, because on the day I was finally determined to start, a beaming American woman came walking down the street with a green cardboard sign announcing free food in the government building next door, a building everyone called, simply, the DIF. We started talking and—what else?—she was a retired kindergarten teacher. I begged her for something to teach, and as instantly smiling and open as she was ever after, Cynta said, "Do you know 'heads, shoulders, knees, and toes'?" Which is how we started the class that first day and every day afterward too.

Imagine it: At the same time as the street cleaning—two o'clock (though now more punctually)—between thirty and forty kids gathered in a semicircle in the place on the block where the sidewalk widened, giggling and jostling and laughing with anticipation as I messed with the speeds of the game song like a faulty record player. First, to gather the crowd, normal speed: all of us touching our heads, shoulders, knees, and toes as we sang the words together in English.

Next, we went slow. Drawing the words out in slow-motion deep voices, dragging with delay: . . . h . . . e . . . a . . . d, sh . . . oul. . . . ders, . . . knee . . . eee . . . eeees, and . . . to . . . o . . . es, until, just before grinding to a complete halt, we'd pick up speed again, singing and touching our heads-shoulders-knees-and-toes faster and faster and faster until the kids were tumbling around on the ground, laughing their heads off.

Within a day or two, parents started to gather around the edges of the pile of collapsed and cackling kids. Later they would help their children draw birds and butterflies and little kid houses with outsized flowers along the sidewalk, which is what we used as a chalkboard. "Head, shol-dors, niiisandtoes," you'd hear the kids teaching their parents as they drew. Then "no,

Mami, *sh*-oldors!" they'd correct. "Ah, okay . . . *ch*-oldors," the parents repeated.

It got so bad that when I sat to meditate in the morning, instead of the mantra I'd used for decades, this new chant, filled with the kids' most startling joy, started up in my heart instead:

> *Head-shoulders-knees-and-toes,*
> *knees-and-toes,*
> *knees-and-toes.*
> *Head-shoulders-knees-and-toes,*
> *Eyes-ears-mouth-and-nose.*

I started trying to get folks to refer to the widest part of the sidewalk as the Museum because of the wild and beautiful drawings the kids left there every afternoon—images of homes, mostly, with trees and flowers and puppies outside. Five-year-old Ema, though, kept drawing simple blue hearts with two little stick figures of "papi y yo" inside them. Daddy and me. Those wonky blue hearts were almost enough to transport a person out of the horror and the pathos of the place—until you learned that Ema's father had been killed two weeks earlier, just before the rest of the family took off for the border.

10

NO ONE THROUGH.

There are whole sections of my notebook in which these are the only words. Page after page after page of the same three words and nothing else written at all:

No one through.

No one through.

No one through.

11

MID-OCTOBER: SIX WEEKS in, and the street was packed full of people everywhere you turned. There was almost no space for new people to lie down and sleep, the heat of the sun remained searing, the cold at night had become piercing, and the increased need for bedding led to tension so high that distributing a van full of emergency mattresses and blankets from El Paso one evening felt like it may have done more harm than good.

But word about the community's cohesiveness had begun to spread by then, too, and a US immigration lawyer from Catholic Legal Immigration Network had started coming to the street regularly to give overviews of the asylum process, which helped. Young, dedicated, and ferociously determined to live life to the fullest, Tania Guerrero had been sent to Juárez for a year from Washington, DC. After months of working with desperate asylum seekers trapped by the border, she knew the system well enough to be able to distill its complexities into words we could all understand, at least a little.

There are five ways you can qualify for asylum, she told the large group of adults that had gathered around her in the place on the street where the kids gathered each day for class. "Only five," she said again, holding her left hand up in the air, fingers splayed, and then folding one finger down with each point as she went slowly through them. You may qualify for asylum, she explained, only if the violence you fear is directed toward you because of: Reason 1 (finger down): your race. Reason 2 (finger down): your religion. Reason 3 (finger down): your nationality. Reason 4 (finger down): your political opinion. Reason 5 (thumb decisively down): your membership in a particular social group. Any violence or harm that doesn't fall into at least one of these categories fails to qualify as cause for asylum in the States, she said twice.

Also, she added, US officials will want to know if you have reported the violence or threats you have received to the police and if not, why not? No, she said, US officials do not necessarily know about the situation with the cartels. And, no, she said again, they do not know, unless you tell them, that you do not feel safe going to the police. You have to explain. And you have to be clear. And you have to be as specific as you possibly can.

Later, when she heard that no one from the community had been allowed to even ask for asylum in six full days, Tania offered to accompany a small group up to the checkpoint at the top of the bridge. It didn't always make a difference, she said honestly, but at least occasionally Border Patrol officers who have been resolute in their no and no and no and no say, when an immigration lawyer is present, suddenly, yes.

The community gathered on the corner across from the chiclet stand to pray. Then Tania led families number one and two on the list up to the checkpoint. They waited up there on the top of the bridge in the searing sun for more than two and a half hours before being told by Border Patrol that there was no room and they had to leave. Tania was furious, quick paced and flushed, when she led the families back to the community on the street. Too frustrated to linger, she promised to come back and try again the next day.

This time Tania's presence did help. And when the families got through, which is to say when they didn't come back to the street, and word spread father to mother, mother to father—*They didn't come back? No, they didn't come back! Then they are through?*—I couldn't help thinking: I'm not an immigration lawyer, only a priest. But if I dress the part, complete with collar and cross, and accompany people up to the checkpoint that way, isn't there a chance that that also might help?

A big-city cop from Guerrero named Ángel and his family were number one on the list by then. Urbane and cool, he had a fluidity and ease that people from the countryside sometimes lacked—a confidence that had led quickly to his being in charge. When I'd wondered aloud with Hector and the small of group of other leaders if my presence at the checkpoint might be helpful, it was Ángel who said, immediately, "Yes, of course. Primero Dios," prompting the others—judicial in their dignity, each one—to nod silently in assent.

But even Ángel grew visibly nervous as the time we agreed on approached. Just before three, he walked to the corner where the community was gathering for prayer carrying nothing at all, while his wife and each one of his children labored under the weight of packs stuffed tight on their backs, and it was as if he didn't know what to do with this lightness. He clasped his hands in front of him as we prayed. Then behind. He rubbed his face. Coughed. Smoothed his pants with the flats of his palms and then coughed again, and when the prayer was finished and someone said, "Wait—Ángel, who has the list now?" he practically sauntered into his tent with apparent relief at the delay.

I'm not sure I'd fully realized before then how terrifying the short walk to the top of the bridge could be. Pressing even as respectfully as this against the edges of the rules required an assertion of self that felt dangerous, and could be lethal, in circumstances like these. In my eagerness for this assertion—and also in the asylum seekers' hesitance—I felt again the vast depths of my entitlement, not individual only but also cultural.

In intense and ambivalent silence, then, we walked up to the checkpoint, Ángel leading his small family in a straight line behind him, me taking up the rear in my collar and my cross, looking as officially clerical as I could. I'd never worn my collar on the street before, and a group of young mothers giggled as they watched me attach it around my neck, then tuck the black bib under my shirt and struggle with the cross that always got caught in the fastenings. They whistled, too, when it was finally on, mimicking catcalls. And the street felt like home then as we laughed together about my getting all dressed up to impress folks with symbols and uniforms that weren't needed there.

But it didn't help much in the end. When we reached the checkpoint, Ángel stepped forward and said, "Buenas tardes, Señores oficiales, somos mexicanos pidiendo asilo." We are Mexicans, asking for asylum. And then we stood and stood and stood and stood in the sun, without shade or water, waiting, until the shift changed, and the new officers repeated what the old officers had said, There is no room, and Ángel finally led us back down the bridge to the street, deflated and hunched.

The next morning, after spending more than an hour praying (ambivalently) for obedience, and (wholeheartedly) for the grace to step out of my blooming self-consciousness at the previous day's failure, I checked in with Ángel to see if he wanted me to accompany them again to the checkpoint. "Yes, of course.

Primero Dios," he said again as if the question itself surprised him, and we made a plan to gather later that day, at one.

The community decided to send two families up this time, and after gathering to pray, we filed through the turnstiles and walked again in somber single file to the top of the bridge. The same group of officers was on duty as the day before, which didn't bode well, but Ángel had his plan and stuck to it.

Once again he stepped forward, along with the father of family number two, and they identified themselves as Mexicans formally asking for asylum. Once again the officers replied, "There is no room. We are full." But this time the younger officer called in to someone on his radio, and less than a minute later, he returned his attention to us and asked how many we were: "Somos seis," Ángel replied, and the officer relayed it into the walkie-talkie: "Six." Then we waited. We were prepared for this: after the previous day's failure, Ángel had been clear we would wait at the top of the bridge unless and until the officers insisted that we leave.

But then a seventh person appeared at the checkpoint and moved to join the group. He was a stranger to us all, and he was dressed in cream from head to foot: cream jeans, cream sweatshirt, cream baseball cap pulled low. One of the officers saw him first and said into his walkie-talkie, "Make that seven."

"No, six," I said, and the officer pointed with his chin to the man in cream. "But he isn't from the community," I said. "And he isn't on the list. And these two families have waited for weeks for this opportunity."

Even with all his urbane fluidity, Ángel looked panic-stricken then, but still I insisted. Addressing the man in cream directly, I told him there was an entire community of people living at the bottom of the bridge, waiting their turn, and that he needed to go speak with them. No one looked at anyone else as I spoke.

The man in cream stared at the ground, Ángel fiddled with the thin plastic packet of papers his wife had given him, and I spun my head back and forth between the two, jabbering, until, after what felt like forever, the man in cream finally raised his head and asked, "There is nothing I can do to get in now?" To which I—God forgive me—said, "Nothing," and he turned and walked back down the bridge.

"Thank you," the officer said. And then, to Ángel, "You can come in," which was pretty much the only thing none of us expected.

Startled, unnerved in an entirely new way because, suddenly, the stakes had just been raised yet again, we hugged quickly, more as a formality than an expression of anything. Then I stood back and watched as the two families of three—father-mother-child, father-mother-child—walked past the orange crowd-control barrier and into the chance of new lives in the States.

"They got through. Thanks be to God—and at last—they got through!" I wrote in my journal when I got home that night, and reading the words now, I feel my breath shift. I had no idea at the time just how dangerous my behavior on the bridge had been that day. No clue that men dressed in fresh cream streetwear like that would almost certainly have come from a place very different from the street at the foot of the bridge, from a place, in fact—and a group—that drove others to the street with their violence.

By saying no to him at that time in that place, I know now that I inserted myself in a world that was still hidden from me at the time. Under the visible and tangible realities on the surface, there was a great palimpsest of others—some of which I sensed, most of which I didn't. It's only now, returning to the scene in my memory from the safety of my home back in Boston, that I let myself feel the fear that Ángel and the others must have felt back then.

"There are just so many layers to reality here," I remember exhaling to a journalist friend from Juárez one evening, thinking, weirdly, of fancy, French-style mille-feuille pastry. Sandra nodded in agreement, smiling wanly. But she was not thinking of mille-feuille pastry.

"Yes," she said. "There are very many layers here, and—like an onion—each one makes you cry."

12

ACCOMPANYING FAMILIES TO the checkpoint at the top of the bridge quickly became part of my daily routine. Every day after class, I'd get together with two or three families from the top of the list, say a prayer with the community that gathered on the corner by the chiclet stand, and then head up the bridge. Collar on, cross visible, I'd wait with them there, hoping that whatever scrap of power I had as an ordained member of the US clergy would help shame or intimidate border officers into doing their duty and letting them through. Sometimes this worked, but mostly it didn't, and three times out of four we'd all return back down the bridge to Juárez—still better odds than when families went up on their own, which is why we kept up with the plan.

Rates of failure like these—eight or nine failures out of ten? twenty-eight or twenty-nine failures out of thirty? seventy-eight or seventy-nine failures out of eighty? more? there was never any way of predicting—meant that families at the top of the list began to be pressured by the rest of the community to approach the checkpoint more and more often each day. After six consecutive days of no movement halfway through the second month, the community voted unanimously that the number one family on the list must approach the checkpoint and formally request asylum every two hours, twenty-four hours a day, until they were through.

Everyone wanted to reach number one on the list, of course. Being number one on the list meant you had hope; meant you were next; meant, after months of nothing but surviving with your family on the packed and chaotic street, that there was, again and at last, some real and actual thing you could do. It was why you were there. But it was becoming clear, too, that being number one on the list was also its own particular kind of hell. Not only must you find the emotional and psychological stamina to gather your family, and everything you own, and walk up—and then down—the bridge, back and forth, back and forth, every two hours, twenty-four hours a day. You had to do it with the entire community watching.

To start with, it was great: the community gathered and prayed, and you felt their support behind you as something real and solid, when your family dropped their pesos into the turnstiles and then walked, single file, up the bridge. If you were lucky and your family was allowed to enter and ask for asylum within a day or two, all was good. But if you were unlucky—if everything came to a grinding halt and you kept going up, and going up, and going up, and going up, and the Border Patrol officers kept saying we are full, try later, we are full . . . well, it was not only your family that started to get tense and then deflated and finally angry; and it was only a question of time before the community decided you were doing something wrong.

People approached me with complaints like this about whoever was at the top of the list pretty much every day, and I did my best to counter them. It is nothing they are doing wrong, I insisted. It's random up there. It has everything to do with the whims of the US system and nothing to do with how the family asks or where they come from. But it didn't take. People listened politely and nodded their heads and then said something like "Still. Someone else should be allowed to try" before walking away.

This was just one more of the effects the randomness of what was still called "the system" had on the community because when your hope rests with America, you cannot turn on America, or your hope will be gone. And hope, at that point, is all you have. At the same time, nothing is happening, you know, and no one is getting through, and someone has to be to blame for the aimlessness and endlessness and powerlessness of waiting and waiting and waiting with so little hope that you could almost go mad.

So you turn on the ones who seem to be failing: the family at the top of the list. If America is the solution, you conclude, the family must be the problem. Perhaps they don't speak well enough, or perhaps they don't understand, or perhaps they are too rural, or too urban, or too simple, or too sophisticated, or perhaps they don't really need to get across as urgently as you do. Whatever the case, the fact is that they are gumming up the system and should step aside and let others try.

A single mother of three in flight from rural Michoacán told me that a group of kids refused to play with her youngest son because he was "holding up the list and not doing it right," she said, and then burst into tears. It had been five days since they'd reached the top of the list, and she was exhausted. I'd first met Cristina when she and another young mother had approached me shyly one morning to ask: please, please, please could I stop using chalk during class?

"I'm so sorry to ask this, Cristi," she'd said, using the same shortened version of my name that she used for herself. "The pictures are beautiful, and the children love making them, but the dust from the chalk gets everywhere, and we don't have enough water to clean." When I assured her that of course we would stop using chalk and then tried to apologize for not thinking of this obvious drawback sooner, her relief was both huge and genuine: "¡Ay, gracias!" she said as if I had just given her something real and important.

This had been lovely, in its way: for once, a real, small problem with a real, small solution. Except later, just after the meeting where it was once again announced that no one had been allowed through, she kind of flung herself down on the curb next to where I was sitting and then burst into tears right in front of the food line. "Another day," she said, several minutes later, wiping her eyes with half of a brown paper napkin. "Another day here with the children. They suffer so much, Cristi—and why? Because of *our* problems. It isn't right."

I tried to counter this rationally, which was dumb, I knew, but I couldn't help it. "It's not because of you," I said. "You are here for them. You are not to blame." And she listened politely, maybe trying to absorb what I was saying, maybe not.

"They cry at night, you know," she said then. "Not all of them. And not every night. But when it is late and most people are asleep, I often hear children crying in the dark. And then it feels . . . well, then it feels . . . impossible."

Cristina had become a regular volunteer during class, and when, on our fourth attempt together, she and her kids were finally allowed through, I felt a tinge of misplaced regret. I would miss her.

Through all this, day by day and family by family, the officers at the top of the bridge began to get to know me—or to recognize me, at least. They'd stiffen when they saw me, and I would too. At the end of the day, when I'd cross back into El Paso on my own for the night, we'd nod to each other as I passed through the checkpoint passport in hand, polite but clearly on opposite sides of something.

One evening, about an hour after a rare successful wait at the checkpoint with a family of seven, an officer I'd never seen before approached me briskly as I walked through the door of the immigration building at the bottom of the US side of the bridge.

"Are you an American citizen?" he asked.

"Yes," I replied, wary as always.

"Can I see your passport, please?" I handed it to him and watched as he turned it sideways, opened it, and then flipped the front page back and forth, back and forth, as if something invisible were hidden there. Then he handed it back to me.

"We are doing some canine training this evening," he said. "Would you mind carrying this briefcase up to the desk?" Half-convinced this was some kind of ruse to get me arrested, I said with as much sense of play as I could muster, "Isn't this the exact thing we are told *not* to do?"

And without even so much as a hint of a smile, the officer said, "I'm a uniformed agent, and I am asking. Please do as I have requested." So I took the case and felt like a dupe.

Up the almost empty line I went, and then down again, up and then down, until a young German Shepherd entered the room from a side door, dragging its handler behind it. Pulling in a straight line directly toward me, the dog stopped three or four inches from the briefcase and started whining and pawing the ground. Its handler crouched down to ruffle its neck and congratulate it. Then the captain returned and, without a word or a glance, took the briefcase back from me and walked away.

Who knows what that was about? Maybe nothing. Maybe something. Either way, though, the tension between me and the officers on the bridge was growing more and more palpable each day, and one afternoon after spending more than five hours up at the checkpoint with two families, it finally came to a head.

The day was typically and searingly hot, and the evening was bitingly cold. I was up at the checkpoint with a young couple and a single mom with two boys. We'd all sat patiently, exposed at the top of the bridge through both the heat of the day and the frigid evening, next to the Border Patrol officers in their shade-providing, wind-blocking tent and in front of the brass plaque with its shiny dividing line: the United States of Mexico on one side, the United States of America on the other.

As had become routine, the heads of each family had announced they were Mexican citizens seeking asylum, and we'd settled into respectful and patient quietness, out of the way, by the edge of the orange crowd-control barrier. We checked in with the officers every forty minutes or so, hoping they'd at least use their walkie-talkies to contact their colleagues at the base of the bridge and ask if—or when—there might be any room.

But they did no such thing. At least not until the shift changed. Then the new officers finally did radio in, and just a few minutes later, a pale, square-shaped man, short and broad, came barreling up the bridge and demanded to speak to me. He was very angry. Not annoyed, not irritated, but visibly enraged. I made sure to read his name tag: Chief Gonzalez, it said.

Ignoring the people I was with, Chief Gonzalez pointed to me and then curled his finger, beckoning me in this way past the barrier into the United States. Without saying a word, he escorted me over to the edge of the sidewalk, where giant loops of razor wire curled maybe twenty feet into the air like an oversized, weaponized slinky. Then he started shouting. Who were these people? he wanted to know. And who was I? Maybe I was new here. Maybe I didn't know just how things worked. But there was a system to manage asylum seekers, and while I may think I was being helpful, if I really wanted to help, I should tell these people to join the Mexican government's list. He said this over and over again: "You want to be useful? Put them in touch with the list!"

All this sent me hurtling back to my very worst, teenaged self (sad but true—would I never learn?), and before I realized what I was doing, I started to counter his claims one by one, trying—and this was the absurd part—to prove him wrong, to win the argument, to switch places with him and become the one who actually knew.

"They should not be on that list. They are Mexican, and that list is not for Mexican citizens," I said.

"Yes, it is!"

"No, that list is for immigrants to Mexico: Central Americans, Cubans, South Americans—"

The results were predictable. Already inflated when he arrived at the checkpoint, Gonzalez pumped up a size every time

I countered, and, shamefully, so did I. Back and forth we went, back and forth: he in his navy blue uniform with the name tag and the bulky, carryall jacket, me in my collar and cross.

"They *can't* work with the Mexican government because they are fleeing for their lives *from* Mexico—do you see?" I insisted and his associate, a heavily made-up female officer who'd hung back until then, joined in the fray.

"Are you saying Mexico is corrupt?" she shouted. "I hope not. I mean, I *truly* hope not." And when she leaned in close to me then, Gonzalez touched her arm to bring her back and then pointed to his collar—reminding her, I guess, that I was wearing one.

That was when I caught myself. Remembering who and where and why I was, I did belatedly what I should have done from the very beginning: made myself smaller than the officers, lowering my voice, shrinking my size, admitting the truth of their superior power the way animals do when the odds are against them. But by then, of course, the damage had been done.

Pulling out his pad, Gonzalez demanded my name, my address, my phone number, and my email.

"Are you paid?" he asked then, which took me by surprise.

"Am I paid? Yes. I am paid as a priest."

"By who?" he asked, adding before I even had time to answer, "Do you work for the Mexican government?"

This was such a strange question, such a seeming non sequitur, that it caught me off guard. I flinched again, this time with confusion, and perhaps Gonzalez lost track of his own logic then, too, because before I had a chance to say anything back, and in the exact same tone he'd been using all along, he announced, "I'll let them through."

"I'm sorry?" I said, thinking I'd misheard.

"I will let these ones through," he repeated, raising his voice again. "But after them, no more," he added with a slicing movement to his own throat. "After these ones, the bridge is closed to them all night—understand? Closed!"

So . . . the five got in. But the whole thing was a bit of a disaster, and I was full of stormy regret. I'd reacted to Gonzalez like a teenager, not a priest, which took a bad situation and of course made it worse. It was incredible to me that I still hadn't learned not to do this. But also, I wanted to add in a whisper, even though, of course, I should and could and—please, God—*will* do it better next time . . . also, the five got through. Which meant the chance, at least, of new lives for a young couple—he a twenty-year-old taxi driver on the run from the cartel, she his eighteen-year-old-wife—and for a single mom with two young boys, a year and a half apart.

But I was worried about the long-term effect of my behavior. Would I now be barred definitively from the ports of entry? Would I be told I had to stop doing the work? By Border Patrol? By the church? Totally possible. If that happened, I would never forgive myself, I knew. How could I be so stupid? But they got through! But at what cost? But five human beings! But what about the rest?

This was how I passed the night, ricocheting between two poles: the truth of those five stepping out of old lives into a real chance at new ones and the fear that I had just exploded the delicate beginnings of real work there.

The next day I wanted to flee from shame when I arrived on the street and discovered that everyone already knew what had happened. Folks approached me almost the second I got there and then gathered around, laughing, wanting to talk about the fight on the bridge, partly proud, partly astonished, partly just plain entertained.

"We won that battle!" one of the leaders, the one with the eye patch who everyone simply called Negrito, said in perfect English, clapping me on the back when he saw me.

"Yes, but what about the war?" I asked too quickly, still anxious and ashamed.

He thought about this for a moment, stroking his chin, pondering my question with mock seriousness before bursting into laughter again.

"And the war as well!" he declared. And I was absolved.

13

IT WASN'T LONG after the community's list was established that people started to be sent back to the street after getting through the checkpoint and spending a few days locked up in immigration detention centers just the other side of the bridge. The first step of the multiyear asylum application process in the United States is known as a credible fear interview. Given by trained asylum officers in the detention centers to which every applicant for asylum from the street was initially sent, these interviews are designed to ascertain whether an applicant's case is at least credible enough to proceed. If it is, an official application for asylum is filed with the US government. If it isn't, the applicant's request for asylum is quickly rejected, and the applicants themselves are tossed back across the border to Mexico.

It's important to remember here that the question isn't only whether danger, or the possibility of death, actually exists. Asylum has never been offered as a general protection against violence. And deprivation alone, even of the most extreme kind, never qualifies. Instead, asylum is granted only if violence is committed, or credible threats of violence are made, against a person because of their race, religion, nationality, political opinion, or membership in a particular social group. This was what Tania Guerrero kept trying to impress on the people on the street. Nothing else counted, she'd say. No matter what.

Still, because the bar was lower at this stage than it would be at a final asylum hearing years later, rates of success for credible fear interviews tended to be high. To begin with at least, roughly two out of every three asylum seekers passed and were released into the United States to pursue their cases through the courts. In 2018, however, a policy named the Migrant Protection Protocols (MPP) was put into place, and since then, all non-Mexican asylum seekers who *passed* their credible fear interviews had been forcibly returned to the southern side of the border and were expected to pursue their asylum cases from there.

Commonly known as the "Remain in Mexico" program, MPP was just another attempt to delay, confuse, and discourage asylum seekers from across the globe. And it worked. Since its passage, even successful applicants for asylum in the United States had now to wait in Mexico, almost always without legal help of any kind, as their cases wound their way slowly through the US courts. In this way, MPP ensured that tens of thousands of people with credible claims for asylum remained trapped in legal limbo, poverty, and its attendant and multiple vulnerabilities in Mexican border cities. For years.

MPP, in other words, didn't protect so much as imperil asylum seekers. It posed such a threat to people's basic human rights, in fact, that it was known along the border not as the Migrant Protection but as the Migrant *Persecution* Protocols. This felt more accurate.

In part because the US government hadn't found a way—yet—to return successful applicants for asylum to the very country from which they were seeking to flee, however, Mexican citizens were not subject to MPP. This meant that those

Mexicans who were able to pass their credible fear interviews continued, most often, to be released into the States and were free to pursue their asylum claims from there.

The community of Mexican asylum seekers on the street, then, wasn't affected by MPP at all. And because many more people passed their credible fear interviews than failed them, it was rare to have applicants returned once they got through the checkpoint at the top of the bridge.

But it did happen. Every now and then, perhaps once every couple of weeks, we'd see families whose success at the checkpoint we'd celebrated several days before walking back across the bridge to Juárez. They'd look exhausted, always, and pale, and lost. Many wore detention center–issued gray sweatpants or sweatshirts, and all were still marked by the centers' color-coded, plasticated paper bracelets identifying them as a health risk, or a mental health risk, or an adult, or a minor.

Regretful and angry sometimes, too, these families never lingered on the street. They'd stay only long enough to tell terrible stories about their experiences in detention before moving on. The holding cells were kept very cold, always, they told people from the community who gathered to meet them. And the lights were kept on twenty-four hours a day, and the food was minimal (and often still frozen on the inside), and the guards— especially the Latinos, they added bitterly—were many times rude and angry and even physical sometimes too.

And after all that, they said—the kids crying and scared and cold and hungry, and the guards shouting and treating even the littlest ones like dirt—the all-important interviews were a joke. Yes, some people passed, they said, but others with stories just as bad—with photographs even, "Look," one man named Jorge said, lifting high the transparent plastic folder he had clenched in his hand—well, we were sent straight out to the van, which carried us back to the bridge and then here. There was no rhyme or reason to it, he said. No logic at all. And it was this randomness—like in all cheap horror movies—that rattled the community most.

It wasn't until the elderly man with the scars and the missing fingers, Martín, was sent back to Juárez, though, that the depth of this randomness began to sink in. One afternoon, a little more than a week after he and his family had crossed through the checkpoint, I saw him arguing with the head of the family that had moved into his large yellow tent on the corner. I hauled him away, calmed him down, and got him some hot food and a drink. Then he broke down in tears and finally told me that his wife was still in detention but that he didn't know where as they had been separated when they'd entered the system. We called the lawyer Tania Guerrero, who called one of her colleagues in the States, who in turn called someone in Washington, DC, and by the end of the day we knew that his wife had, for reasons unknown, been moved to a detention center in Alabama.

Martín, of course, was distraught. And he was not the only one. He told me that a doctor who worked in the facility in which he'd been held—someone who'd seen the gunshot wounds in his belly, the severed fingers, the scar across the top of his head—had become visibly enraged when he learned that Martín was returning to Mexico. The doctor had shouted so loudly and spoken so quickly that the translator couldn't always keep up, Martín said. But one thing he repeated often enough for the translator to get was "That's it! That's it! I can't do this anymore!" The doctor pushed a pile of papers off his desk, then stormed across the room and slammed the clinic door. "I quit!" he said, and, crying then, begged Martín to appeal. "Please fight this, please!" he said. "I will help you."

People on the street were unnerved by Martín's return. He drank too much sometimes and became unpredictable when he did, occasionally venting his frustration and fear and unwilling displacement onto the community. But he was one of the most obvious candidates for asylum as well. If he'd been sent back, then literally anyone could be.

As a crowd grew around him, peppering him with questions—some about how he was and what they could do to help, others only about what he had been asked and what it was, exactly, that had allowed them to send him back—I went off around the corner to read a handful of papers he'd given me, trying to understand how it had happened.

Here are some excerpts from the transcript of his credible fear interview:

> Why do you fear returning to your country?
> *I fear that I will be killed.*
> Who do you fear?
> *Cartel(----).*
> Anyone else?
> *No. Just the cartel.*
> Have you ever been physically harmed in your country?
> *Yes, they kidnapped me one time. Kept me three days.*

Physical harm?

In three days 20 times about. They thought they killed me.

Is there anyone, any entity in your country, e.g. government officials such as the police, who could protect you from these people?

In Mexico there is no police who is legal.

What do you think would happen if you did file a report with the police?

They will kill me that same day if I file a report.

Who?

The cartel.

Would the police protect you?

No. Never.

Why not?

Because they work for the cartel, the whole police from Michoacán.

If the police doesn't protect the people and is not "legal," why does the cartel fear that you will tell on them to the police?

The police work for them. They have Michoacán divided. One for (----) Cartel. One for (----) Cartel.

Did you or anyone, e.g. in your family, ever file a report with the police?

No. No one ever files a report. It is the same thing as if you are going to be handed to them.

How do you know?

It is a small town. At the beginning people made reports. Then they disappeared.

Have you ever seen the police with the cartel?

Yes. One time they closed the street. On both sides of the street there was patrol cars, blocking the street. In the middle there was an exchange house, where they exchange pesos for dollars. Members of the cartel were breaking the door down with axes, officers were blocking the street so they could do the job.

Did they try to stop the cartel?

They were trying to help the cartel.

What is the national entity that protects your country?

The National Guard.

Can National Guard protect you?

No.

Do you believe the government of your country would harm you or allow you to be harmed if you returned to your country?

Yes.

Do you believe public officials would look the other way if they saw the person/people you fear harming you?

Yes.

Do you fear harm by any public officials, such as the police or anyone connected to the government in your country?

Yes.

Why?

Because it is the same, the government and the cartel.

14

CITY OFFICIALS STARTED to water the grass in the park by the next bridge down, where another large group of Mexican asylum seekers had camped, and it was clear that this had more to do with trying to scatter the community than with any concern for plant life.

People used to do the same thing in Boston, I remembered, hosing down steps and alcoves and patches of sidewalk each morning in order to move along homeless people who'd spent the night there. It's the same with park benches too. If you stop and look at them for a minute, you'll realize that those nice metal armrests at their centers aren't there so much for your comfort as to prevent people from lying down and making a bed of them at night. And as I lay in my own bed in El Paso, unable to sleep as I was always unable to sleep back then, I began to wonder just how much of life seemed to be one thing when it was really something else altogether. I mean, how much of what seems to be good and generous and kind is really an act of self-interest or something undertaken for the profit of another? "Doing good is a hustle too," my old friend and mentor Debbie Little used to say. And it was true, I knew. Doing good is a hustle—and being seen to do good is that same hustle squared.

The church falls prey to this temptation particularly hard. Like magpies, we are drawn to the sparkle of grand ministries and shiny new programs even as, too often, we hurry past the complexity and vast mystery of the actual human beings they supposedly serve in our rush to promote and display them.

I'm susceptible to this also, of course. As days went by, I found myself increasingly quick to turn from the terror of the mom who tapped me urgently on the shoulder and then handed me a ziplock bag holding three crusted syringes ("There are children everywhere here, Cristi; please tell someone," she said and then wept and wept and wept without stopping and without words); and even from the beauty of a large group of kids kicked back against the curb, sharing a bag of candies so spicy they had to wave their hands in front of their faces and suck cooling air into their mouths through gaps in their teeth.

Instead, I'd started to spend hours on the paperwork I'd become convinced I must do to birth "an effective new ministry" on the border. The Diocese of the Rio Grande had agreed to establish this new ministry, and this was both a relief and a boon. But it also meant that I had to spend hours with folks in El Paso, talking about the "effectiveness" and "demonstrable impact" of the ministry—when all the time, of course, that mom and those kids *were* the ministry. Each one of them carried both the truth and the effect of our nation's policies in their bodies. And each one of them deserved the kind of time and care that can only come when all thoughts of ministry, or effectiveness, or funding are absent.

The task in front of me, I kept trying to remind myself, was not so much to "build something"—though that could sometimes be important—as simply to *remain*. To remain open, specifically, to the layered and horrifying truths on the ground, as well as to my own (complex, always various) humanity in the face of the (equally complex and various) humanity of every person I met. This kind of openness is hard enough to maintain anywhere. But in a world where inhumanity reigned, where personhood was unilaterally and preemptively denied, and so where cruelty abounded, it was, I think, the hardest thing of all. But it was all that mattered in the end—at least for me.

"The Word became flesh," after all. Not "the Word became programming." Or "the Word became ministry." Or "the Word became justice," or "fairness," or "freedom," even. The Word is now and has always been all these things, for sure. But to save us, to show us a way out of the traps we ourselves lay, day after day after day, the Word actually became *flesh* . . . and dwelled among us.

I tried to remember this, to hold it clear and bright in the center of my desire. Often I failed, and then I almost drowned in a sinking kind of double fear: of the tangible horror that was everywhere, obviously, but also of fleeing from that horror too soon and so failing to find the life buried deep in its center. There were also plenty of days, though—or plenty of moments within days, at least—when that life suddenly opened out in front of me and invited me in. And the truth is that these moments almost never had anything to do with the macro-mission at hand. Instead, they had to do simply with the God-given worth and mind-blowing beauty of each and every plain old human being.

They were tiny, always, these glimpses behind the veil—minuscule, impossible to see from even a few feet away. And while they were sometimes searing in their single-pointedness, they were often more diffuse as well—more like a tub of warm water than a sharp strike of lightning.

Half an hour after class one day, for example, a mother brought her six-year-old son, Jonathan, to me, almost literally by the scruff of his neck, and said, "My son says he was first in the class today. Is this true?"

There was no such thing as an official "first in the class" on the street, of course. Instead, everyone was first—each in their own, particular way. But something important was going on between Jonathan and his mother, and after looking from her to him and then back again, I narrowed this truth and said, "Yes. It is true. Today Jonathan was first."

His mother's body visibly drained of its anger then, and she turned to him with a sudden rush of pride and embraced him, which in turn allowed him to embrace her, a child again. For a minute or so they stood together there, mother and son, wrapped in each other's arms, holding each other up. And moments later I left, happy that I was, all of a sudden and however unlikely, in the position of being maestra—teacher—out there on the street. Because no matter what happened in the immigration world that day—what rights were stripped away or confounding new policies implemented; no matter who got through from the street or didn't get through; who was sent back or broke down on the edge of the sidewalk into sobs of despair, or horror, or sustained, desperate exhaustion—Jonathan was first in the class that day, and his mother could breathe, and so could he.

It happened in class all the time too. The kids were so openly and visibly thirsty for our gathering every day: for the fun, of course, and the normalcy of at least one reliable thing happening at the same time in the same place, but also and more deeply for the focused, one-on-one upholding of their goodness, their number oneness, best-in-class nature, every one of them.

    We still didn't actually teach much. We played lotería with English words, and we sang head-shoulders-knees-and-toes, messing around with the speeds still to make it more fun. Most days we sang a learn-your-colors-in-English song, too, with Cynta's handmade drawings of sky and grass and flowers ("What color is the sky?" "It's blue, it's blue, it's blue!"). And then we'd finally settle down to do some drawing—on sheets of fresh white paper now with crayons instead of chalk—and the quiet that descended then was transcendent.

    Slowly, and with a settled depth of concentration that astonished me every time, the kids drew whatever was asked: 1 yellow sun, 2 green houses, 3 purple dogs, 4 orange bugs, 5 blue kitties. When their page was full, they'd come creeping up to me, one by one, and hand me their paper, and as quietly and intently and specifically as I could, I'd exclaim over the beauty that was there. Then I'd take them through each element of their work to the tune of "What Color Is the Sky?"—What color is this bird? What color is this house? What color is this dog, or tree, or butterfly, or sun? And one by one, they sang their answers back to me: "Eeets bloo, eeets bloo, eets bloooooo," but so quietly, the connection between us absolute, like a prayer.

    I was almost overwhelmingly aware of the weight my words carried as I responded to them then, which was partly why I, too, spoke so quietly. It was something new, something born on the street, this weight. And something to do only with children and only with them one on one. With great care then, and with all the attention I was capable of, I continued until we were done: "What color is this grass?" whispering the answer to them when they didn't know it—"green." And they repeated "greeeen." Or "brown," "browwwwwn." Or "orange," "oraaaange." And with these words, we met.

It felt like Holy Communion. It *was* like Holy Communion, at least insofar as it was the only other time in my life I'd ever been approached with such a clear request/demand/desire and had been able to fill it exactly. God, not me. Love buried deep within and also free beyond human specifics, endless and real and no matter what.

15

They already died fifty years ago. These were the words that kept me from sleeping as I lay on the bottom bunk in Sister Betty's room the weekend she and Peter invited me to stay at their house. *They died* decades *ago!* And it was true, in a way; they had. Sister Betty and Father Peter had taken lifelong vows of poverty, chastity, and obedience back in the 1950s, and since then, they'd neither sought nor seemed to need comfort, personal safety, separation from the sufferings of poverty, or security of any kind at all. They gave all that up forever ago, leaving them free to work wherever they were most needed because this was the life they had chosen and sworn to uphold: faithfulness and love and solidarity with the poor and the suffering of this world in imitation of the one they sought to follow, Jesus-who-is-love.

Willingly forsaking wealth, power, success, security, and even your own freedom to choose, once and for all, is a profoundly countercultural approach to life in this world at this time. And while many who make these same vows remain fearful and cramped and as beset by greed for all kinds of comfort as the rest of us, the result of Peter and Betty's faithfulness was both clear and undeniable: peace and joy and the kind of openness that great cleansing winds blew through strongly enough to hit even me in the face.

I'd never met anyone like them.

Friday nights, for example, they had "Whatever You Want Night." On the Friday I spent with them, this ninety-six-year-old man and eighty-seven-year-old woman had been going full steam from six in the morning when they held a prayer service with their neighbors. Then they headed out, at about eight, for their weekly peace protest in front of the El Paso town hall, large banners and placards in hand. After that, they went to visit a sister of Betty's, Sister Bea, who, at eighty-seven, helped run one of the busiest shelters for newly arrived migrants in downtown El Paso. There they subjected themselves to a long, fractious interview with a journalist from Voice of America ("Voice of America?" Peter exclaimed when I told him who the reporter with the big camera had been. "But they're the enemy!"). Finally, they returned back over the bridge to Juárez and visited the street to offer blessings to members of the community there who'd been asking for a Catholic priest.

When word that he'd arrived began to spread, a group of people gathered around Peter with both reverence and need. They answered his quiet questions, telling him just as quietly, and with an open kind of gentleness that belied the subject, about the violence from which they were fleeing. They used words like *kidnapping*, and *murder*, and *extortion*, and *rape*. Peter and Betty listened intently and without saying a word for more than twenty minutes in the hot sun, and when the storytelling finally dissolved into silence, Peter took off the white baseball cap with a picture of Oscar Romero on the front, which he always wore, and told them in fluent Spanish that this man, too, had been threatened by people with power. Archbishop

Romero had stood with those who were poor and suffering in his own country, El Salvador, he told them, and because of this, he, too, was killed—in church, right in the middle of mass. Romero was officially beatified by the Catholic Church in 2013, Peter said, replacing the hat carefully on his head—adding that the people, of course, had known he was a saint for years before that.

"San Romero de Latino America," Peter repeated, musing a little, and the people listened, and absorbed, and for a few moments there was the silence that comes from a deep sense of being seen and understood. Afterward, when Peter made tiny signs of the cross on people's foreheads, their faces shone with all they were receiving.

Only after all this, did Peter and Betty bring me back to their place across town. It was very hot in the house, and Peter walked right through the green curtain into what they called the "men's dorm" to change into a pair of shorts, while Betty cleared the oil cloth–covered table in the kitchen. A few minutes later, once Peter had pulled out their tiny TV and settled into his ancient, hard-backed chair (which had just been beautifully repaired, he told me, stroking the wooden arm), Betty approached from the kitchen and announced the beginning of "Whatever You Want Night." Then she leaned in and added more quietly, "Peter, want me to tell you what we have? We have a slice of pizza—It's lasted such a long time because it was so big, she explained to me on the side—or eggs if you want an egg sandwich, or cheese if you'd prefer a cheese sandwich, and to drink we have Coke and water and wine." Here she paused, as if to take stock, and then beamed, genuinely overwhelmed. "Yes," she said, filled with wonder and astonishment. "We have all that!" and the words shot straight into my heart.

"We have all that!" True wealth, right?

It was the same on the street, of course. Despite their poverty, or perhaps because of it, the community seemed perpetually ready to share what they had. Almost as soon as they arrived, they started welcoming other kinds of desperate people into the relative protection of their communal life on the street. The first was an elderly man, gaunt and frail-looking, who'd turned up at the afternoon meeting asking for food. He had been fed, housed, and cared for by the community ever since. Out of gratitude, he'd taken to sweeping the sidewalk up and down the block every day, and as he made his way slowly up the street with his broom one afternoon, he and I got to chatting about his crippling back pain. I offered to share some medicine a doctor friend back in Boston had prescribed for my own back pain, and we agreed I should leave it inside the flap of his tiniest of all tiny tents if he wasn't there the following day when I arrived. Just before we parted, I said, with my usual apology, "I'm so sorry. Will you remind me, again, of your name?" At which point he looked at me, genuinely surprised, raised his arms in disbelief, and told me, simply and as if it was so self-evident as to be almost a joke, "¡Soy Jesús!"

I'm not sure, but I think I gasped out loud then. I know I held my hands to my cheeks and blushed. Jesus. Of course. He was the least, even there—the almost invisible one in the miniature tent made in the United States for children to play with.

It is only true to say also that the community just barely tolerated the particular idiosyncrasies of too frail Jesús and his even more frail partner, María, who joined him soon after. But another man they took in, a windshield washer with a drinking problem named Jaime, was beloved. A man with the energy of about forty people crammed into his tiny frame, Jaime was always a bit bouncy on the tops of his toes, ready to pounce, or change direction, or leap, or spin, or flip on a dime. Energy like that was rare on the street, and almost as soon as he moved in, he started to help welcome people, leading them to one of the leaders and then helping them settle in. Almost every evening he organized a flamboyant soccer game for the kids on the street, too, and within days of showing up, Jaime had become essential to the community. Both guide and follower, both native and outsider, he became a kind of focal point. The one people turned to. The one who knew.

Then one day, apropos of nothing and entirely out of the blue, he collapsed. First he sat down. Then he lay back on the sidewalk, shook a bit, and lost consciousness. His eyes, half open, showed only white. "Jaime! Jaime!" we called, but he didn't respond. "Jaime! Jaime!" Belén splashed cold water on his face: nothing. Humberto slapped his cheek: nothing. I thrust my phone into someone's hand, asked them to call an ambulance, and tried to shoo the kids away. We all thought he had died.

Belén, the first female leader on the street, turned away and started to cry then, head in hands. But then someone else found a heartbeat. He's alive! He's alive! they shouted, and, quickly, we turned Jaime on his side, placed a backpack under his head, and I silently started to pray. A few seconds later, he opened his eyes and sat up.

"I'm fine, I'm fine," he said, sitting up straighter now on the curb. "Don't worry. It's happened to me since I was a boy. I have fits. Honestly, I'm fine . . . I really am fine."

Belén offered him both her hands, hauled him up to his feet, and then carefully led him across the street to the entrance to her tent, where she wrapped him in a full body hug and burst into tears on his shoulder.

But almost exactly one week later, it happened again. Just before the afternoon meeting and right next to the water stand, Jaime simply crumpled onto the sidewalk, felled by something unseen. Again we poured water on his face and across his lips, and again we grew scared. I set my timer. Five minutes more of this and we would call the ambulance. But he came around a couple of minutes before then. With help, he sat up again on the curb and, dazed a bit, began to fill out.

More practiced the second time, parents had shooed most of the kids away by then. But Alejandro—a stalwart nine-year-old from Guerrero who couldn't hear and couldn't speak and who, through the raw, surging power of his unfiltered life force, caused so much trouble in this community of otherwise pliant kids—would not be moved. No matter how many times people told him to leave, he stayed right where he was, standing in front of Jaime like a sentry. Firm and undemanding in the way of all the people and especially of the men in this little community, he was willing, it seemed, to wait that way forever.

As soon as Jaime was alert enough, Alejandro caught his eye, tilted his head to the side, made his eyes roll around in their sockets and his arms shake, and then stopped and looked at Jaime with a big question mark of a shrug. Clearly a question: Are you okay? Jaime nodded and made a thumbs-up sign: I'm okay. But this wasn't enough. More quickly this time, Alejandro again tilted his head and rolled his eyes and shook his arms up and down and then "came to" with a question mark face and a thumbs-up sign. Again, Jaime nodded, yes, yes, and gave the thumbs-up. Partly relieved, and partly still worried, Alejandro made a heart sign with his two hands and then pointed at Jaime. Jaime almost fell over again just from the force of that. Instead, he made a heart sign and pointed back at Alejandro. And the two of them stayed like that, pointing to each other with this strange, silent, focused seriousness before making the heart shapes again.

For what felt like hours, this was how it went between them: pointing—heart; pointing—heart; pointing—until Alejandro couldn't be still anymore. Letting his hands drop suddenly, he stepped toward Jaime once, twice, and then crumpled like a dropped puppet. Jaime grabbed hold of him then and clung as if the small boy were a life preserver. For a couple of minutes the two of them rocked together there, this nine-year-old child who was from far away and could neither hear nor speak, just barely standing in the street, and this man who was a drinker and a street person sitting on the curb, in each other's arms, openly weeping now. And those of us who got to see it felt the world tilt up on a slant and then vanish for a moment as the Spirit coursed through us all.

Small, real things. Small, real things. This is what I kept trying to remember and to trust. Not big, impressive things but small, real things are the way to love—with, through, and for the other. Small not because we can't be bothered but because we are small ourselves. And because every time we honor this smallness without shutting down—every time we acknowledge our lack of sufficiency and remain willing, even so, to both meet and be met by the other—well, whatever follows then will both come from and lead to the realm of abundance some of us call God. And real transformation will happen, only on an infinitesimal scale. This is how small, real things make a (small, real) difference.

And this is important too: because small, real things are necessarily incarnate, they cannot be faked, or sold, or even advertised. They can only be sought in the moment and then welcomed. They require nothing flashy, nothing expensive. Only a mute and muscularly passive stance, full of willingness and reliability and vulnerability.

It isn't that small, real things don't sometimes become large, real things, because they do. It isn't the smallness that's the point but the intention. It's as if the act of desiring and then seeking something small liberates us to receive without measure. As if by not aiming for bigness—or for success—we somehow become freed from the regular marketplace world, in which something is always given in exchange for something else, and enter instead a realm where giving and receiving become the same thing.

Here are a couple of sentences by Sandra Cisneros which cheered me up one dark night in El Paso because they say more or less the same thing, only more simply. "I don't know anything," she writes. "But I know this: whatever is done with love, in the name of others, without self-gain, whatever is done with the heart on behalf of someone or something . . . whatever work we make with complete humility, will always come out beautifully, and something more valuable than fame or money will come. This I know."

16

No one through.

No one through.

No one through.

No one through.

17

THERE IS NO room. I am so sorry, but we are full. It would be dangerous for you—and for us—to let you in. Right now there is no space. It is against the law to let in more than the fire marshals allow. No. Not right now. We are full. Come back at two. Come back at five. Come back tomorrow at dawn, or at ten, or at twelve, or at three. Try later. Or wait. Yes, it is your right to wait. Yes, it is your right to come back. We can't let you in now. We are full.

It was always the same.

First, the approach: the stuffing of the backpacks until they were solid as stones, then the gathering of the children, the prayer, the somber walk to the bridge, the passing through the turnstiles, three pesos in each, and the stop at the bathroom at the bottom where, every time, one kid changed their mind deciding they actually *do* need to pee just as everyone else is coming out. Then the wait again, nerves fraying, and the regrouping, the nodding to each other like the nods of altar servers—*Are you ready? I am ready*—and then the uphill, single-file walk to the top of the bridge, always, always, always in silence.

"Yes?" the Border Patrol officers in their crisp navy uniforms asked the worn, now adrenaline-pumped asylum seekers as they approached the place where Mexico became the United States. Or "Documents, please," which—every time—prompted the request, "We are Mexicans seeking asylum. We are afraid for our lives," and then the response, "We are full. There is no space. We have no room. Try again at six; try at nine; try at eleven; or at two."

Except, of course, there was room. And there was space. And it would not have been illegal for those officers to let the asylum seekers in. In fact, it was illegal for them not to. I'd long known this theoretically, of course. It was what metering was all about. But one mid-October night I learned that in El Paso alone there were hundreds of beds available right then, that very day, in a giant tent Border Patrol had opened the summer before.

No one knew exactly how much room there was in the tent because all information of that kind was resolutely withheld from the public. But the structure, which officials called the "soft-sided facility," could hold as many as fifteen hundred people, and since MPP had taken hold, it had been operating way below capacity. "It's not *completely* empty," a US immigration journalist told me in a bar. "I mean, there are people there. But it's far from what it was prior to MPP, and there is plenty of room. Plenty."

I'd driven past that enormous white tent many times since arriving in El Paso without having any idea what it was. The news that there were, right then, rows and rows and rows and rows of empty beds, just waiting for asylum seekers who never came . . . well, after days and weeks up on the bridge hearing the same lie from officers, male and female, tall and short, young and old, kind and extraordinarily crude . . . well, it felt sort of like someone slapped me hard across the face and then punched me in the stomach for good measure.

There *was* room.

But still the people continued to come, and I was increasingly becoming the person who first explained how things were out on the street when they arrived. I told a single mother who'd just gotten off the bus from Guerrero with her four young children, and was seeing for the first time the almost six hundred men, women, and children crammed along two sidewalks of one city block, that we had had a full week without anyone being allowed to even request asylum. A few minutes later I had to nod my head and add that yes, when and if she *did* finally have a chance to request asylum for herself, it was likely ("again, yes, I am sorry, likely") that her two youngest—both toddlers, both US citizens—would be separated from her.

I told her these things on the corner, by the currency exchange, as a family of thirty arrived all at once from Michoacán. Also dismayed by what they saw, they simply came to a halt in the middle of the road, faces blank. About five seconds later and without consultation or second thought of any kind, the older man, bent under a duffel bag towering high over his head, who seemed to be in charge, announced they were leaving again. I have no idea where that family went. All I could do was call Cristina Coronado and then wait with the single mother and her two tiny kids until a van came to take them to a hostel for the night, even as—all the while and at the exact same time—a bunch of kids were playing tag in the street, and someone somewhere had a radio going, and women, young mothers mostly, were sitting together on a stack of blankets piled into a sagging kind of sofa halfway down the block, laughing behind their hands in that hidden way they had, light and fresh.

This was just how things were. Beauty and horror and fear and laughter and despair and hope were all exposed out there on the street, spinning around each other like an overpacked load of colors in a dryer so that from one minute to the next—one *second* to the next—there was never any telling which would become visible.

It wasn't just the community of asylum seekers who defined the mood, of course. Unlike the tent encampments at the other bridges, we were lodged in the middle of downtown Juárez. This meant that all day long, local people going to work or heading for the bridge, and street vendors, and drunks, and addicts, and tourists, and random passersby keen to see what was happening, threaded their way through the block. Some gave dollar bills to the children or candies. Others brought bulging black garbage bags of cast-off clothing or iceboxes filled with homemade food to give away. Still others picked their way carefully through the community with an air of disdain and hissed out words like, and this is a quote, "The yanquis should drop a bomb on this street and clear the whole place out." And underneath all the surface movement and change and noise, of course, great cycles of violence and trauma swirled as thickly as the dust that was everywhere.

One morning, Belén brought over a young man visibly disoriented from grief and helped him settle in next to me on the curb. Silently—literally, without a single word—this young man pulled out his phone, leaned over toward me, and began scrolling through photo after photo after photo of the remains of his slaughtered family: sprawled and bleeding in the kitchen, slumped in the living room, splayed in the bedroom. I wanted to close my eyes. I did not want to see. But as the only thing in the world I could do was stay there and look, I tried as hard as I could to do just that. He didn't speak as he scrolled, the young man; he said nothing but the names of the people he loved whose remains were now too brightly captured on his phone's small screen. And for what felt like forever I simply sat there, nodding and repeating these names in a way I hoped might echo through him like a prayer as he wept.

This man, too, had to join the list, and move into a tent, and wait out on the street for who knew how long—weeks certainly, months likely—before being allowed, perhaps, to ask for asylum in the States. And through it all, the community met and organized themselves and walked politely up the bridge and politely back down multiple times a day, making sure they did nothing that might rankle or upset or cause any problems to anyone with power. "Primero Dios," they continued to say. And "Si, si, primero Dios," I would respond, trying to match their faith step by step, when what I really wanted to do was scream, "Enough of this orderliness—create a racket! Make a scene! Charge the bridge!"

I fantasized about this silently for hours each day, and while I'd managed to resist so far, I wasn't sure how much longer I'd be able to hold out. Patience, patience, I'd tell myself. And hush, hush. Dare not to speak, not to do, not to try to fix. Receive and receive and receive and say no-no-no-no to the chant of your own ego, every minute of every hour of every day. I'd never been very good at surrendering myself in this way, but I was learning. And to help me, the adverse effects of the "help" offered by well-meaning people—people who simply could not deal with the truth of the suffering they saw—were becoming increasingly common and plain to see.

Mostly they were tiny and harmless enough: The American priest who met his first asylum seeker in Juárez and was able to listen to the elderly woman's anguish for just a minute and a half before straightening up and taking control, full of advice for the woman, who had spent three months on the road already and almost six weeks more right there on the street, as if he were the one who knew. Or the anonymous person who cooked a mountain of chicken for the community but who then—out of fear, or thoughtlessness, or shyness, who knows?—simply left it all on the corner in a see-through plastic bag with only the word *pollo*, "chicken," written on a note card taped to the top. This led, in the end, to a wrenching but unanimous decision to throw it all away—because who knew how long it had been sitting there, and who wanted to risk it?—and to the tears of multiple kids who wanted to eat it anyway.

Sometimes, though, panicked responses to the suffering of others reaped real harm. One afternoon a young man set up a table under a rainbow-striped beach umbrella at the bend in the street by the bus stop. He had a shiny red battery-operated megaphone, and through this he announced that he was there to help. He had forms required by the United States for the asylum process, he said. They were in English, but he would translate them and then help folks fill them in. "Take a form," he announced, handing them out. "Take a form." By the time I arrived, a long line extended down the block, and people were nervous.

Tania, the lawyer from Catholic Legal Services, had been visiting the community regularly for a couple of months by then. She was knowledgeable, immensely capable, and deeply committed—and she had never mentioned these forms. So, a bit worried, I introduced myself to the young man at his table and asked if he was a lawyer.

"No, I am not a lawyer," he said.

"Oh," I responded. "Do you work with lawyers?"

"I do not," he replied. "And I don't have to. I looked up what is required on the internet. These forms are completely legitimate. Look, it says right here: *Application for Asylum and for Withholding of Removal*—I mean, why is no one helping them?" he interrupted himself to ask then. "And why are they stuck out here on the street? It's just not okay that they're not allowed to go to a shelter!"

"We beg folks to go to a shelter all the time," I tried to explain, but he was too disgusted to hear. I called Tania, filled her in, and then held up my phone to the mic on the young man's megaphone so she could speak to the community directly.

"Listen to me," Tania said, her voice crackling doubly through the phone and the megaphone. "Do not fill out these papers. They are real forms, and they come from the United States—this is true. But they are for later in the process—for *after*, not *before*, the credible fear interviews you will be facing when you cross. Do not fill them out now. Doing so can do you real harm."

False claims of expertise were not new on the street. Just the week before, a man claiming to be an immigration expert distributed pages he said revealed new US asylum policies. The pages were topped with blurred copies of the Immigration and Customs Enforcement insignia and were full of randomly selected paragraphs from immigration-related academic study papers. But because it was all in English, the package looked official enough at first glance, and several people on the street were considering paying the one thousand pesos he asked for. It was only when Belén asked me to (at least sort of) translate a couple of paragraphs during the afternoon meeting that everyone realized the package was a fake and moved on with the same kind of regretful but unsurprised stoicism I was seeing again now.

Disappointed but resigned, people began returning their clean-as-new forms to the young man under the beach umbrella, leaving them in neat piles on his table. One couple stayed with him there, though, and the young man continued to work with them even then, continuing to offer his misguided assistance not because he was bad but because he was good. He was good, and he was tender, and he simply could not handle his own powerlessness in the face of so much pain and real suffering in others.

And he was me, of course. This young man with his hair pulled into a knot on the top of his head, and his beach umbrella, and his shiny great megaphone, and his desire to do good: he was a perfect caricature of the me who screamed silently away all day that I needed to do something, and take control, and get things done, and fix all this!

But there was another me, too, one who insisted more quietly that my work was essentially anti-dramatic and so, also, often, anti-gratifying. The opposite of the grand gesture, this type of work took time, and restraint, and poverty. It had to be, in the end, birthed by the desire to learn, not to teach; to become, not to shape; to love unconditionally and endlessly because I am also loved unconditionally and endlessly. And this—as I said to myself, over and over then, and am still saying even now—this largely involves frustration and grief and a seemingly endless repetition of tiny, finite, pointless-seeming tasks and always, always a reflection back to others of their own beauty and strength and power instead of projecting my imaginary own onto them.

Jesus has plenty to say about this. And St. Paul too. And if I needed further bolstering—which I did, always—so did the recently resigned secretary of defense, General Mattis, of all people. Browsing a profile of him in the *Atlantic* later that same evening, I discovered the following astonishing summary of George Washington's leadership style: "Washington's idea of leadership," Mattis said, "was that first you listen, then you learn, then you help, and only then do you lead. It's a somewhat boring progression, but it's useful."

18

TWO DAYS AFTER the man with his forms created so much confusion, Tania brought a team of lawyers who were visiting from across the States for an unplanned and additional charla, or chat, on the street. They spoke with the community, clarifying again the fundamental requirements for asylum; visited one of our classes for the kids; and then offered to accompany a couple of families up to the checkpoint.

Initially, a crowd huddled in the shade, trying to decide how many people should go up with the team. Two families? Three? When they finally agreed to go with three, the call went out, echoing down the street: "¡Familias 1, 2 y 3!" "¡Familias 1, 2 y 3!" until the three families emerged, ducking under the flaps of their little houses, packs stuffed tight as stones on their backs, caps pulled low—except Luis, the rakish kid who always wore his baseball cap sideways and did that day, too, though he was visibly terrified under it, as they all were.

It had been so long since anyone had gotten through—eight full days of trying and failing, trying and failing, trying and failing—and the hope the presence of the lawyers brought undid us all. A prayer came easily—for God's mercy to fill the hearts of the Border Patrol, for God's courage to fill the three families, and for God's grace to course through everyone who would not get through today, bringing them what they needed in ways that they could actually feel.

Afterward I crouched down to speak more intimately with Luis and the other two kids. I needed to express something to them, to imbue them with some urgent thing, and it turned out to be this: how extraordinary they were, and how lucky my country was that they were hoping to move there, and, most of all, that however hard the next few days may be, they had all they needed already, right there in their hearts.

The intensity with which the kids listened to all this was sobering to the point of silencing. Stunned a bit by it, and wanting also to arm them again for the reality that awaited, I lumbered back up to my feet and gently cuffed Luis's jaunty, sideways cap the way I always did. But he just kept looking at me, and looking at me, until he turned to follow his family single file up through the turnstiles and onto the bridge. We were all openly weeping by then. Even sharp-cheeked Francisco, the sinewy blond leader whose family was now next on the list, had tears streaming down his face and at least partly because we all needed space to subdue both our hope and our fears, we quickly dispersed.

Hoping for a few minutes of solitude, I set off for the black-and-white coffee shop on Juárez Ave, where I'd become a regular. But another little boy, Samuel, far smaller than Luis and without the pizzazz, stopped me as I passed. He'd been trying to speak to me earlier, and I'd told him then that he needed to wait. So here he was again now, silent in front of me, with his even littler sister and his only-just-taller mom.

I stopped, crouched down again to be at eye level with him, and waited. For a time the three of them just stood there in a straight line: little boy, tiny girl, slightly taller mom. Then Samuel began to tell me what he'd been trying to tell me all afternoon. That his mother was afraid. That she had heard that the kids would be separated from her in detention and that they would be inside for months and months; and it would be freezing; and they'd have nothing to keep themselves warm and not enough to eat; and if either of the children—he or his sister, he said, looking down at his sister for a moment—started to cry for any reason, or maybe even to squabble, that the guards would come in and beat them and then take them away.

Was this true? he asked, this boy who looked maybe seven and who was speaking already so lucidly and fluently on behalf of his mother, who was too afraid to speak, even to me. This was what his mother had heard, he repeated. This was what people had told her: that they would be separated, even if they made just one mistake.

I can't describe the intense effect this tiny boy speaking like a man on behalf of his terrified mother had on me. He stood so straight. And he spoke so quietly, and also so clearly, because it was important what he was saying, he knew, and he might not get another chance, and he didn't want to forget anything.

"Is it true that me and my sister will be sent to live with strangers?" he asked then.

"Do you have family over there?" I asked.

"Yes."

"Then you will all probably go and live with them together."

"But they live in *Orlandoflorida!*" he anguished, as if it were the real name of hell, or maybe only Pluto or Mars—it was hard to tell. I tried to let him know that every kid in the world wanted to go to Orlando, Florida, because that was where Disney World was, but I don't think he'd ever heard of Disney.

"Mickey Mouse lives there," I said stupidly, turning to his little sister. "And Donald Duck."

"Does Little Pony live there too? I love Little Pony," his sister said.

"Yes, Little Pony too," I said, and still the boy stood there, straight and as tall as he could make himself, asking his questions, voicing the fears of his family.

I told him then that I was a priest and was therefore not allowed to lie, not ever, and that I had never heard of children being separated from their mother because they cried or squabbled, or of them being beaten. But it was not enough. It was as if Samuel was waiting for something.

And then all of a sudden I knew what it was. I took off the bracelet I'd been wearing every day, the one Judy back in Boston had given me that read *Though She Be But Small She Is Fierce*, and I wrapped it around his wrist, pressing the metal ends together so they touched around his tiny arm, telling him as I did so what it said. I added that the adults might take it away from him in detention but that they would have to give it back when he left to go to Orlando, Florida, and that it didn't matter anyway whether he had it or not because it was true what it said: he was fierce. And he already had everything he needed in his heart.

I pointed to his heart then, and then to his sister's heart, and to his mother's heart, and told him that God lived in there—God!—and that no one could ever take God away. Ever.

The intensity between us then must have been palpable because a silent and creeping group of wide-eyed little kids had started to gather around us. So I pointed to each of their hearts, too, one by one, and very quietly told each one of them the same: God is in here. God is in here. God is in here. God is in here . . . and then I had to leave because I really was going to utterly, utterly lose it.

When I returned to the street the next day, I learned quickly that all three families who'd gone up to the checkpoint with the lawyers made it through—and that sharp-cheeked Francisco and his family had too. They'd waited a couple of hours, then gone up the bridge at ten thirty and never come back. The mood was ebullient. Counting Francisco's, four families through in one day!

There was an energy, a buoyancy along the street that had almost completely vanished until then. It was visible. And audible too. Instead of hiding away in their tents, people were out on the sidewalks, greeting each other with words and with smiles instead of with a muted kind of blankness. And the kids! The five kids of the family that was now so suddenly number one on the list were giddily, jubilantly spending all the change they'd been given by passersby on candy because, they said, the officials over there would only throw it away when they crossed.

"They won't throw it away," their parents countered. "No one throws money away!" But by their glances toward me as they spoke, I realized they weren't sure this was true. Anything was possible over there—maybe even money would be treated like trash.

But there is more. Because minutes after I arrived, young Samuel found me again. He showed none of the excitement of the rest of the community. Serious, almost somber, he asked if I would come to his mother's tent. When I agreed, he led me through the garbage-bag flap that served as a door with the same strange combination of intimacy and formality he'd shown me the day before and then settled on a flattened piece of cardboard next to his mother. I sat down opposite him, straight-backed as he was, still and silent as he was. And then he began to speak. His bracelet—the one Judy had given me and I then gave him—was still wrapped around his wrist, and he fiddled with it every now and then. Otherwise he was entirely still—except for his words, which flowed, unobstructed, from his core, through his mouth, out to me.

His mother was still scared, he said in the same direct, deep-eyed way as before. So scared that she wanted to return to their home. But he did not want to return. He wanted to wait. He wanted to stay, and then to cross over, and finally to see his father in the United States because he had only communicated with his father on the phone since he was six. And that was not right.

"How old are you now?" I asked then, as gently as I could.

"I am eleven years old," he said, as if it was essential that I understood.

His mother smiled at me then and scooped up his little sister. Very quietly, as if not wanting to interrupt, she tucked herself and her daughter under the black plastic flap and left, giving us both the space, and Samuel the privacy, to talk. And he did talk—fluently, evenly, and entirely without passion or pause—about his deepest hopes and his deepest fears until it became clear that what he feared most was exactly what was going to happen.

They were returning home, he said. His father had already sent across money for the bus tickets, and they were leaving tomorrow at noon. There was no work for his mother to do at home, and the school had long ago closed because no one let their children out of their houses anymore—"Not since kids, little kids," he said, "started being kidnapped. Not since then."

It was true that his father called regularly when they were home, but every time he did, his parents fought. She thought he had a new woman up there in America, while he insisted he was only working hard, struggling to pay the rent, and eat, and keep his car going, and send money home. And then they'd start screaming at each other, and his mother would hang up the phone, and, again, he would have lost the chance to speak to his father. And he didn't like that. And he didn't want that. And he didn't think that was right. He needed to be able to speak freely to his father. And they needed him with them to be safe.

This was why they were there now: to cross over, and reunite with his father, and in this way to be safe. And they were so close—just across the bridge from the United States! All they had to do was wait a little more until their number was called. But his mother was too afraid: afraid of the night, afraid of the community, afraid of detention, afraid of America. She did not need to be afraid, but she was. He himself wanted to wait and believed waiting was the right thing to do. Otherwise one day, maybe soon and maybe not so soon but for sure *one* day, they would just have to start the journey over again. Because one thing was clear to all of them: they needed to be safe. And to be safe, they needed to be together. This was what was important, for his sister and him to have a mother and a father, and for them to be together, safe where they lived, without having to worry about being kidnapped or being shot or being hurt, and this was important for his mother also. He'd had dreams about him and his sister going to school in America, he said then. But that would not happen now.

And with that, the words stopped. He had said all that he had to say.

Neither of us moved. He sat still, and so did I. It was my turn to speak, I knew, and I had no idea what to say. His life was making a U-turn away from what he longed for and toward what he dreaded, and there was nothing in the world he could do about it. Not one single thing. So what in the world could I possibly say? Quietly, evenly, not wanting to break the connection that still held us firm, I took a deep breath and did what I always do when I don't have a clue: simply opened my mouth and trusted that the Spirit would speak.

"Sometimes life is very, very hard," I heard myself saying then. "During these times, everything that is hardest and worst and most wrong-feeling is what happens. And when we are children, there is nothing we can do about it. Which is terrible. And painful. And maybe even wrong. But it isn't the end of the story," I said. "You are eleven now. And one day, not too far away, you will be a young man. And then you can make your own choices and live your own life. If you still want to, you can return here to the border and try to reunite with your father or live your life in whatever way you think best.

"Whatever you decide, though, the truth is that there is something extraordinary inside you," I told him again, touching the place where his heart was. "Something truly extraordinary. And while that might make things more difficult for you now, it will make many things possible in years to come—and then you will do amazing things, Samuel, not for yourself only but also for your family and for your country—for both of your countries, perhaps."

Then I upped the flame between us, turned the knob all the way to ten, and said with a voice I barely recognized, "And one thing more, Samuel. Do not ever forget what I am telling you. Never forget it. You are extraordinary. And you have everything you need deep within you. And you've only got to wait a few more years before you can start being and becoming the person you were born to be."

Then I nodded, and he nodded, and as mysteriously as it had started, it finished. There was nothing more to say.

I don't remember now how I left the tent or what happened between then and the time I got home—though I left Juárez for the day straight after. All I really knew was that Samuel, who was Jesus, was alive, right there and right then, in a tent made of garbage bags, on the edge of the Paso del Norte bridge, in Ciudad Juárez, in the heat. And that Samuel, who was Jesus—who is all of us—was yet again on the way to a place he did not wish to go. For now.

19

A LITTLE MORE about Samuel.

A little more because once again I remember—how many times is it possible for one person to forget?—that this is all that there is, all that can be hoped for: Union. Release. Encounter with the essence of the other in ways that free us from the confines of our own particular time and our own particular place and release us instead into eternity.

Mystics and teachers of the church write about this kind of thing all the time. Most often they do so in the context of silent and solitary prayer. They talk about union as the result of a process of turning away, of saying no, and then no, and then no again to the distractions of the world, and of silencing and stilling ourselves in that which lies beyond. This practice has been central to my own life, and I'll never be done being grateful for it.

But I've long known that this depth of reality can be found not only by turning away and saying no but also by turning toward and saying yes—to Samuel in this case, and his eyes, and his voice speaking so evenly about the truest, transient specifics of his own finite life.

Again, eternity—which is Love, which is God—dwells not only outside the specifics of this world but also deep inside them. And whenever one person is able to fully share themselves with another, it's as if a key turns in a secret door, which then bursts open with the force of this usually hidden world, annihilating in its brightness and also fulfilling in its gentleness.

It is almost impossible to find words for this, at least words that make sense. The only one I can find is *prayer*, which is why, whenever someone asks me how I pray, I want to reply, "By meeting others." Most often, something stops me from saying this, though, and I rattle on instead about my morning practice: I read about the saints, I say, and listen to the Gospel, and spend time in silence. Occasionally, something shuts down in the other person when I do this, as if they can tell that I'm not really paying attention, that I'm not really hearing what they are asking.

So today, at least, I want to try to be clear. I am able to pray most deeply when I stop praying all together; when I'm out in the world, vulnerable and worn; and when the last thing I'm thinking about is prayer, or God, or anything in the least bit religious. I am able most deeply to pray when all I am thinking of is the person in front of me.

This is why if this encounter with Samuel was the only reality I managed to enter on the border, my entire stay would still have been worth it. Tiny, hidden, and at the same time surging with life, a meeting like this is the kingdom of heaven: a few grains of yeast in a mountain of flour, a tiny seed with a giant great mustard tree inside, a young boy with a middle-aged woman in a homemade tent by the Paso del Norte bridge. It is everywhere, all the time, this unity, this freedom, this love. Closer to us than our own breath, it is now. And now. And now.

20

No one through.

No one through.

No one through.

21

THE CONFERENCE ABOUT the church and the border that I'd registered for months before—the one that hadn't felt like enough back in Boston—was about to start. I'd been asked to preach during the opening worship, and feeling certain that this, too, was part of my work—which is to say, part of why I was on the border in the first place—I had agreed. It would be the first time I had left the community since it had begun, and I told the community leaders—at that time Belén, Juan Carlos, and Matías—that I'd be gone for a three-day weekend on a dry day when the dust was blowing.

"So you are abandoning us," Juan Carlos said, unflinching.

"Yes," I replied, doing my best to be as unflinching as he, and looked right back at him, eye to eye. "I am. I am abandoning you. And I will be back on Sunday."

I imagined I'd think about this exchange all the way to Arizona. But I didn't. Instead I thought about nothing at all, which was confusing, even at the time. The stupor set in almost the minute I climbed into the van. Canon Lee was driving, leaving me free to fold into the all-the-way backseat and drift into the desert landscape outside like a kid, while he and two bishops chatted up front.

We were entering a landscape I'd only ever seen on TV: a technicolor, cowboy Western set of huge blue skies and little shrubs and striated mountains with flat tops. When we stopped at a lonely gas station, it was so quiet, so deeply silent, that I was startled at one point by the crisp crack of a crow wing flap overhead. And the scale of everything! Magnificent. Empty. Arresting. Most of me couldn't shake the notion that none of it was real, and a small part of me kept trying to bring together this make-believe place with the cramped, concrete reality I'd just left behind. But I couldn't do that either. I couldn't do anything really, except gaze.

I thought this strange and passive state would pass when we arrived, but it didn't. I fell asleep almost as soon as we got to the motel and spent hours the following morning stretched out in bed, then sitting on a bench outside, and then walking—so slowly, I could get up no speed at all—from my room to the van, from the van to my room. Other than that, nothing. I was barely present at all, and even so it felt good. Because, so far from the community, it was possible. Because, so far from the community, nothing was expected of me.

I was at the conference in part because I'd finally sent a proposal to the diocese seeking approval for what I was by then calling a "small, nimble chaplaincy" on the border. *Chaplaincy* has come to be associated largely with religious work in hospitals or prisons or colleges, but it is actually a term used to describe any work of the church outside of its regular structures. I used it intentionally in the context of the border to signal that the work there, too, would be rooted out in the world rather than tucked away from it, and also to make it clear that—like all chaplaincies everywhere—the work on the street would focus not on teaching or instructing or advising but on the kind of willed and sustained openness to the reality of others that comes from seeking to *be with* rather than to fix, and to learn rather than to teach. Accompaniment, being present, being available, seeking to help in whatever ways were possible once the needs for that help became clear: these were to be the touchstones of the work. And the diocese went for it.

A month or so earlier, Lee had brought the bishop to the street so he could see what the work actually looked like on the ground. And while I tend to be a little strained—and strange—when I get around bishops, Bishop Michael seemed relieved to be out in the world and grateful to be in a place where being a bishop wasn't quite so confining. He was clearly moved by the grace and dignity of the people on the street, too, and after a couple of hours of talking and listening and praying with them, both he and Lee readily agreed to accompany a family of six up to the checkpoint.

As always, the community had gathered to pray before passing through the turnstiles and walking solemnly up to the top of the bridge. Once the formal request for asylum had been made and then denied, and the family gathered out of the way to wait, huddled up against the wire mesh fence at the edge of the bridge, I watched the bishop settle into the silent, ravaging process of absorbing it all: the desperation, and the suffering, and the pain, and the frustration, and the beauty, and the love that is mingled together into a wordless whole up there—all bounded by powerlessness so entire it can feel hard to breathe. I'd felt sure he'd give up and leave after just a few minutes. But they stayed for four hours in the end, the bishop and the canon, being treated specially by no one and doing nothing more grand or impressive than offering their presence to a woman named Berenice and her five children, who had been number one on the list for nine days by then, climbing to the top of the bridge every two hours, twenty-four hours a day.

Four hours is nothing, of course. But four hours is also everything, and I got the impression that the bishop liked being there and would have stayed even longer. Did he get annoyed? Yes. Did he shut down a bit and get bored? Yes. But that is all part of it. And still he stayed, watching and listening and absorbing it all—especially, that day, the wanton generosity of a clarinet-playing beggar who wove through the traffic making music for change and who kept spending the pennies he earned on candies and little savory snacks for the kids of the family we were with.

"Have you seen what he's doing?" the bishop asked Lee at one point. "He is literally spending every penny he makes on the children!"

Later, still clearly transfixed, he said, "I'm going to give him a blessing. You think that's okay, to offer him a blessing?"

"Of course!" Lee replied. And for the next five minutes the Texan bishop, in his oversized, black cowboy hat and clerical collar and fancy black suit, and the Mexican beggar, in his knockoff sweatshirt and rolled-up pants, huddled together on the bridge, bowed head to bowed head, holding hands.

When the bishop came back to us afterward, his face shone—and five minutes after that he went quietly down to the office at the bottom of the US side of the bridge to "find someone to talk to," he said. Then, out of nowhere and after nine days of trying and failing, trying and failing, Berenice and her children were finally let through.

For a time, this had felt like a breakthrough, like the church and the world had come together in a way that was less generalized, or cozy, or spiritualized than usual. And in a certain sense this was true. The diocese was now fully behind the incarnate, messy, often thankless-feeling work that we were by then calling The Bridge Chaplaincy. A church close to the border was willing to serve as a kind of focal point for this new, cross-border ministry, and I had agreed to stay until funds had been raised to keep it all going for at least a year and a more long-term, ideally locally based replacement could be found. Besides, with the bishop's accompaniment at the checkpoint, we'd met institutionalized power with institutionalized power and—for once, and with a directness and lack of fanfare that are rare in the church—we had prevailed.

At the conference, though, the church and the border seemed, again, as incompatible as ever. And as I mingled with priests and laypeople and visiting bishops and guest speakers, I felt every bit as lost in the comfort and certainty there as I ever had in the discomfort and confusion on the street by the bridge. It was difficult to keep it together enough to preach during the gathering's opening worship service, but I did—just. The minute I returned to my seat, though: tears and tears and tears that felt like they would never stop.

Worshipping with others in a church again had something to do with these tears, I knew. The physical act of it, I mean: sitting in a pew, and bowing to the cross, and singing the *Kyrie*—Lord have mercy, Christ have mercy, Lord have mercy—with hundreds of others who were doing the same. I'd felt met by the liturgy of the church like this from the very beginning, as if the sounds and communal actions of worship resonated in my body, welcoming me in my flesh, even as my flesh welcomed it. It was at least part of the reason I'd felt so drawn to the whole Christian project in the first place.

But peeling even the edge of the Band-Aid off the pain and grief and searing, US-sponsored inhumanity on the border as I preached had something to do with it, too, and afterward it was as if I could not find a bandage big enough to seal it all away again. I couldn't find words that made sense. I couldn't find scenes, or stories, or ideas, or themes, or theologies, or cohering statements of any kind at all, in fact. And for the first time in a long time, the silent, screaming longing that sometimes stands in for all that—or perhaps that chases it all away—took hold of me instead, flinging me internally from dead end to dead end, with tears.

I couldn't leave the sanctuary when the service was over, that's all I knew. Instead, I settled into an empty pew and tried to regroup by breathing slowly, deeply in and deeply out. When Bishop Michael happened to walk by, I asked if he had a minute and then followed him over to a quiet aisle on the side. There I asked, apropos of nothing, if he knew why the clarinet player from the bridge spent all his time begging for change. No, he said. He didn't.

"Because his father needs a wheelchair. He can't move without one. He is no longer able to leave the house at all," I told the bishop, which is what the clarinet player himself had told me. "But I don't even know if that's true," I said then, crying again. "And I haven't passed on the information to you because of that. But now I have. And now you know."

The bishop looked concerned, also a little confounded.

"A wheelchair!" I almost shouted then. "Any old kind of wheelchair! That's why he's out there. Now you know." Then I slapped him on the back and walked away.

22

I RETURNED TO find that it had rained all weekend on the street, and that—on their own and under cover of night—Alejandro, the nine-year-old who could neither hear nor speak, and his exhausted, asthmatic mother had managed to get through.

The community had figured out that when it was very late, and raining, and also very cold, the Border Patrol officers occasionally left the checkpoint to huddle in the dry warmth of their cars, parked behind loops of razor wire just alongside it. And of all the people in the community, it was young Alejandro and his often-despairing mother who first used this knowledge to get through.

I'd been gone when this happened, but I found it easy to imagine how it went: the depressed, determined mother and her difficult and inspiring child agreeing, in their own made-up sign language, in their tent, in the rain, in the middle of the night, that yes: yes, they would go—and fast! Alejandro would have double-checked this because he always double-checked everything, whirling his hands round each other in front of his chest—the way he did when he wanted "head shoulders knees and toes" to go faster and faster—and his mother agreeing: yes—fast!

Decision made, they would have left their tent at three in the morning in the pouring rain and marched quickly together down the street, through the turnstiles, and up the bridge to the checkpoint. Thrusting chin, eyes fixed, fists pumping, entirely determined, putting all that anger to work for once, Alejandro would have been ahead of his mother, I'm certain of it. And after a quick glance to confirm that the checkpoint was deserted, he would have reached for her arm and then led her on past the orange barrier, down the bridge, through the rain and the cold and the darkness, without letting his mother slow or stop, until they reached the office building on the other side, where they could—finally, after years of abuse and more than two months living out on the street—ask for the protection of the United States of America.

It was hard to believe but true nonetheless: a nine-year-old boy who couldn't hear or speak and his worn-out, too-soon-aged mother got the better of the US immigration system and forced our country to uphold our own laws. This was gospel topsy-turviness at its very, very best, and I thrilled at the news.

Other than this, though, the unusual levels of rain had been hard on the community. Most families' structures were too flimsy to reliably keep anyone dry. Babies were getting sick with coughs and fevers. One had blood coming out of her nose. Summer was shifting at last to fall, and it was starting to get cold, too, especially once shade engulfed the street in the early afternoons. If the heat had led to a kind of crouching avoidance, the cold was bringing on a sharper response, one that felt almost like fear. No one had the right gear, or anything like it, and that first week back, chamarra, chamarra—jacket, jacket—became my mantra.

The kids came first, of course. Cristina and Sigrid and the folks from St. Christopher's and from St. Francis's across the border brought trunk loads of miniature winter jackets in bright pinks and blues, and small winter boots, and beanies, about forty of which featured the sticking-up ears or pointy snouts and long whiskers of northern woodland animals.

The increasing cold was making it harder for the kids to keep focus during class on the street as well. Cynta suggested we move to an indoor space around the corner, where members of her church had been cooking for the community once a week, but I was reluctant. Almost everyone on the street had seen and known things neither Cynta nor I had ever seen or known, and we needed to be almost extravagantly respectful of that. Trusting their kids to us for an hour on the street was one thing; sending them to a building out of sight was something else altogether.

She was right, though. It was getting too cold to ask kids to sit and listen to stories and draw comfortably outside. When I brought up the idea at an afternoon meeting at the end of my first week back, parents were both quick and unanimous in their decision. "¡Por supuesto, Cristi, sí!" they said, and we made the move straight away.

This meant that at two every afternoon, the teaching team now walked up and down the street like any other salespeople hawking their wares. "¡Clase! Clase de inglés," we'd chant, "¡Es hora de la clase de inglés!" And one by one the kids would emerge from their tents, or turn to their parents to ask if they could come, or run down the street, pushing each other around and laughing, or rumble down the sidewalk on a hollow-wheeled, plastic trike someone had dropped off as a donation. We still gathered in the place where the sidewalk widened, but now, once everyone had arrived, we did two new things. We lined up, and we took a vote.

It was always the same, this vote, and the question was this: How shall we cross the street to the classroom today? On the road? Or on the red metal pedestrian bridge? Every day the vote was unanimous: *The bridge!* And then, every day, one child changed their mind: "No! By the street, by the street!" they'd say, but they were only doing it for the fun.

Parents were still an essential part of the teaching team, and several came each day—mostly mothers but some fathers also, and once we had posted an adult at the top of the line, we'd wind our way to the small, pedestrian bridge. We couldn't run up there, but we could stamp our feet on the shiny red walkway and pretend we were a train. Then, if we liked, and if we were making enough noise to unite us and the mood took us over suddenly, we could join in a song my grandmother had made up lifetimes ago, in Havana. She wrote many songs, my grandmother—one for each of her children, one for mosquitos, one for birthdays, and for hope, and for storms, and for missing home.

This one was simply called "El Tren," and it went like this:

> *Chuc chuc chuc chuc, ya el tren se va*
> *Chuc chuc chuc chuc se va p'allá*
> *Si te quieres montar apúrate*
> *Si te quieres montar, apúrate . . .*
>
> *Choo choo choo choo, the train is leaving*
> *Choo choo choo choo, it's on its way*
> *Hurry up if you want to get on,*
> *Hurry up if you want to get on . . .*

Faster and faster we'd sing it, as we clung to each other's shoulders and stamped our feet against the red metal bridge and whistled like a train. And it became a kind of prayer, of course, a chant, perhaps even a psalm, communal and uplifting and enabling of time travel the way all real prayers do, joining, in this case, my grandmother, who'd fled to the United States from Cuba more than sixty years before, with these kids I was starting to love so much in Juárez at the tail end of 2019. My heart nearly burst every time.

And here are some lines from another psalm, this one from the ancient psalter people have been using as a prayer book pretty much continuously for the past five thousand years:

> *Though the cords of the wicked ensnare them, they do not forget your law.*
> *Redeem them from human oppression, that we may all keep your precepts.*
> *Those who persecute them with evil purpose draw near,*
> *They are far from your law.*
> *Salvation is far from the wicked, for they do not seek your statutes,*
> *I look at the faithless with disgust.*

Reading these words in bed one morning, after yet another week with no one getting through, led me deep back into my anger at the bridge: not the shiny red metal one, of course, but the militarized gray one, guarded by officers with guns, and leash-straining dogs, and tracking devices, and razor wire. I copied the lines into my notebook, grateful as always for the breadth and depth of these ancient prayers and for their wide-open embrace of humanity and of me, even at my worst. (That word: *disgust*!)

All day, whenever I was between things, I pulled it out and read it through a few times. And by the time I accompanied a family of six to the checkpoint late one afternoon, it, too, had become a chant-prayer. Powerful and true and therefore strengthening, it whittled itself down to just two lines:

> *Though the cords of the wicked ensnare them, they do not forget your law.*
> *Redeem them from human oppression, that we may all keep your precepts.*

I repeated these lines silently, over and over, as we waited at the top of the bridge.

> *Though the cords of the wicked ensnare them, they do not forget your law.*
> *Redeem them from human oppression, that we may all keep your precepts.*

> *Though the cords of the wicked ensnare them, they do not forget your law.*
> *Redeem them from human oppression, that we may all keep your precepts.*

By the time we failed—again—and then separated, the family returning to their tent on the street in Juárez, me to my apartment in El Paso, the two lines had reduced again to just one.

> *Redeem them from human oppression, that we may all keep your precepts,* I prayed.

And again:

> Redeem them from human oppression, that we
> may all keep your precepts.

I hung on to that line for weeks, repeating it whenever there was nothing else to say, even to myself—which was every day, at least once. After the giddy rush of success with the visiting lawyers and Alejandro and his mother's miraculous breakthrough, the border had shut tight again, and the mood in the community was becoming increasingly bleak. Samuel and his family had gone, returned to their hometown, where violence and death were practically the norm. Martín was still waiting for word of his wife and two other members of his family who were spread out in detention centers across the American South. The weather was turning, upping the tension and reducing any hope of even momentary comfort or ease. And no one at all had gotten through the checkpoint for eight full days.

The record, from way back, was ten days without success, and it looked as if we were approaching that again. Hope was falling away, revealing what was always there, just underneath: frustration and fear and exhaustion and despair. A phone had been stolen. Also two pairs of shoes and some sweaters. Things felt—again—like they were beginning to crumble.

Only time spent in class offered any kind of reliable respite: an hour or so of thinking about shapes and colors and playdough and tape instead of violence and flight and survival and death. But by mid-November the stress was starting to show even there. One young girl, Magdalena, started to cry every time she began to draw, always a picture of home; a boy named Dylan charged round and round the space as if sitting still might undo him; and tiny María Elena spent most of every class in her own private world, writing letters to her people back home in a miniature pad she always carried with her. Close to the beginning of class, she'd turn to sit sideways on the bench so that her bent left leg made an almost private workspace. Then she'd flip open her pad and, clutching her pencil firmly, begin to dictate quietly to herself as she wrote.

"Querida Lesli," she whispered one afternoon as the rest of the class was listening to Adriana's mother read a Spanish language version of *Caps for Sale*, "te extraño." "Dear Lesli, I miss you. I hope you are taking care of Peki and Poki and that you are good." María Elena was five years old, and she was as focused as if she were an executive in a law firm on the twenty-third floor someplace, taking her own dictation. I slid into the seat next to her. Lesli, she told me, was her cousin. And she really did miss her very much. Her dogs too. And her house. And her grandmother.

I asked if I could read the letter she'd written, and she beamed as she handed it to me, proud to share the neatly lined page of impeccable, imaginary scribble writing. Legible only to her, those wiggly lines of longing and hope were as pure a prayer as I have ever seen.

Tendrils of loss, grief, and longing had always been present in class, of course. How could they not? But they were growing more visible with each passing week now. One afternoon, Cynta had everyone make their own self-portrait, and while most of the faces the kids colored were light and sweet, a few were genuinely disturbing: one was colored solid gray, another was covered in thick black scribble, and a third had its eyes and mouth scrubbed out in red.

Even Adriana, a usually well-behaved girl whose mother was a teacher from Guerrero and now helped out regularly in class, had started showing her frustration, overwhelming kids with her sheer and unyielding determination to have this pair of scissors or that set of stencils. Often only her mother could calm her down by placing her hands gently on her shoulders and then leaning in close so that the tips of their noses almost touched in a kind of soft nuzzle.

And yet the resilient joy of the kids remained too. And it was by harnessing this hope and energy that the little classes developed a reality all their own. The teaching team had grown by then to include two wonderful American women who had appeared on the street more or less by chance and decided to stick around. Kathy, a former nun and retired school principal, and Crystal, a lifelong activist who'd lived in Central America for years, both knew how to hold a room full of kids, and their regular presence helped broaden the activities we were able to offer.

Just a couple of weeks after moving indoors and thanks entirely to volunteers from Cynta's church, we were able to open a small library. We presorted books into beginner, intermediate, and older-kid categories and, at the end of class each day, laid out a selection from each on benches for the children to choose from. One six-year-old, Alejandro—who never took off his brown bear hat, which featured two rounded ears up top and long arms with paws at the sides that could be used as a scarf—showed me how he'd taught himself to read by tracing any words he found with the long-ago broken and still-bent tip of his right forefinger and then mouthing them out loud, syllable by syllable ("kuh—ah—rro: ¡Carro!").

Like many of the kids, Alejandro was a little awed by the responsibility of caring for a book overnight. A few days after we first "opened" the library and after a heavy rain, a young girl's mother came to me, deeply distressed because the book her daughter borrowed had gotten wet. It was dry again now, she said, handing it to me. But—see?—the pages were still curled at the edges, and her daughter was so ashamed she was refusing to come to class.

From then on we added great, long talks about the inevitability of wear on the books and how much more important it was that a book be read than be protected. But some anxiety remained, and I suspect that Alejandro was one of the few who read the small pile of books he borrowed every night, cover to cover. He liked nonfiction books about animals best and read one about polar bears, and one about frogs, and one about dogs, and horses, and ladybugs, and monkeys. He told me how many times he'd read the latest each day ("Five times!" he'd say, splaying his fingers wide: "Five!") and then, as if to prove it, settled in to read a few pages out loud to me every day before class really got going, following his bent finger haltingly along the page.

It didn't take much to sustain the enthusiasm of the kids, which in turn sustained us. One day when Cynta wasn't there, I panicked that I didn't have enough material to engage the kids. We ended up falling back on one of the photocopy-ready lesson plans I'd ordered from Amazon months before and made ice cream sundaes out of paper. For about an hour we cut, colored, and pasted bowls and scoops and bananas and whipped cream and nuts and cherries and then stuck them all onto brightly colored construction paper and hung them on the wall. As class was ending and the kids were lining up for the trip back over the shiny red bridge to the street, Alejandro brought his paper ice cream sundae to me and said, "Mira, Maestra: I wrote *yomi-yomi* at the top! *Yomi-yomi!*" he said again and then fell about laughing with the same delighted joy he'd have if a real bowl of ice cream sat there in front of him.

What was this life force that renewed and renewed and renewed? To enter the kingdom of heaven, you have to become like children, Jesus told a bunch of grownups who wanted to know. Is this what he meant?

It was the same with so many of them. No matter the depth of horror, or despair, or fear, or grief that swept through the street as regularly as day turned to night, the kids continued to—what is the word? Resist? Yes. They continued to resist in the most powerful way imaginable: with joy and laughter and love.

Even on the day the community broke the record and went eleven days with no one getting through, they would not be cowed. All day long, Alejandro; his best friend, Dylan; and a fiery young girl named Juliana kept trying to interest me in the wounded pigeon they were hoping to coax back to health with water-soaked Saltines. "Come, Maestra, come!" they said, grabbing my hand and pulling me across the street, away from the adults who were arguing about how and who and when to go up to the bridge. And again: "Come! We have something to show you." And they did.

Tucked inside a cardboard box lined with a soft blue blanket the kids had scavenged from somewhere, the rescued pigeon was trembling. Hushed suddenly, and somber, the three of them huddled around the box and peered in, taking turns to comb softly through her feathers with the tips of their fingers in order to calm her. Her name was Tingy, they told me. And she could not fly.

23

COMMUNITY LEADERS ROSE as slowly up the list as everyone else, and each time one of them made it across the border, the community selected another to replace them. They were taxi drivers and small business owners and construction workers and farmers unwilling to forsake all they'd worked for to the ever-increasing demands of the narcos. Genuinely heroic, most of them were burdened with the kind of straightforward and stubborn conviction in justice that had led to their need to flee. Some had already lost a family member. Others had received the kind of death threat they couldn't ignore. Almost all had made choices requiring levels of bravery I'd never before seen. And now, together, they were keeping this large community peaceful and orderly and buoyed. Nothing good that happened could have happened without them.

Once though (or, possibly, twice?) more skilled maneuverers rose up to become leaders as well—people who could read a crowd and know, instantly, where its weak spots were, especially where the list was concerned. The community was so perpetually in flux—families arriving, families getting through, families giving up and going back home, or to stay with relatives in another state, or trying their luck at another port of entry, or crossing illegally with a pollero—that empty spaces frequently appeared on the list, spaces that could be sold for relatively large sums of money. Corruption was inevitable.

The newest leader, Víctor, was openly disgusted by this. Day after day he'd publicly check—and then recheck—the list during afternoon meetings. When he invited me into his tent to talk privately one afternoon, I was pretty sure why. It was only the second time I'd been invited inside someone's tent and, remembering Samuel, I took off my shoes as I crouched low under the tarp flap to enter. Víctor was a builder by trade, and I was astonished by the ingenuity and scale of his family's temporary home. Deep, wide, and bathed in light diffused through layers of blue tarp, the roof was high and variously angled, and every inch of interior space was dry. There was even a window made by a clever piece of folding, which, he showed me, was closable at night.

Another member of the leadership team, Homero, was already there when I arrived, sitting cross-legged on a triple-folded blanket, and for a time the three of us tried, awkwardly, to settle beneath the nervousness we all felt. Corruption was not something people talked about, at least not above a whisper, because corruption was tethered to money, and money was tethered to violence, and violence, too often, was tethered to official and publicly sanctioned power and so to impunity—which cycled right back to corruption again and to the systems that had driven many of the people to the bridge in the first place.

Even I had heard rumors about people buying numbers on the list from one of the leaders by then though, as well as stories about families who'd given up on getting through to the US selling their numbers to new arrivals on the street. A few days before, I'd also learned that at least a handful of the Mexican officials in beige uniforms who supervised the turnstiles at the base of the bridge were charging two hundred dollars to "assist" a family seeking asylum. I never figured out exactly how this worked. All I knew was that whole families would be hidden in the women's bathrooms at the base of the bridge until "the time was right," when they were escorted up to the checkpoint and were "helped through." Endlessly naive, I had been outraged when I'd heard this.

"Something has to be done!" I'd said, which prompted the friend who'd told me all this to grow firm and clear, the way a frightened parent is firm and clear with their overzealous and naively opinionated teenager. "There is nothing you can do about it, Cristina," she told me, sitting on a low wall across from the giant pink cross where we'd settled to share a bowl of steaming hot corn. "You cannot get involved. It is too dangerous. Act as if you do not know. Do nothing—and do it visibly."

Yet here now was Víctor, already forced to flee with his family after organizing workers to oppose increases in narco protection rates, trying—again!—to do something. Careful throughout our meeting to refer only obliquely to specific incidents and actual people, he said he'd grown so sick of what he'd been seeing with the list that he'd called a meeting with leaders from the other two communities at the Libre and Zaragoza bridges. This was how Víctor learned that in addition to their own list governing access to the checkpoint, every family in the park at the base of Puente Libre was now being given an individual card, or ficha, by that community's leadership. Each ficha was numbered and dated by hand, and the names of every adult in the family, along with the number of kids, were written clearly on the front before the whole thing was sealed with sticky-backed plastic. When a family got to be number one on the list, they were required to show their ficha, along with a photo ID, before approaching the bridge, effectively reducing the chance of someone else taking their place to something like zero.

This system of individually stamped fichas was what Víctor now wanted to replicate. He asked if I could get them a stamp for this purpose, which, of course, I agreed to do, and as I made to leave his tent, Víctor reached into one of the bags that served as furniture in his blue tarp home and very carefully, with both hands, took out an embroidered huipil from its place at the top. "We want you to have this," he said as he handed the embroidered blouse over to me, formal and serious and gentle all at once.

The blouse was stunning, its deep, magenta base almost entirely covered with elaborately woven flowers and leaves and vines. I was stopped by it, completely taken aback and unsure what to do.

"We want you to have it," he said again.

"It's too much," I replied. "You should bring it with you to the States."

"Please," he said extending his arm to offer it again. Realizing that while accepting it was all wrong, not accepting it would be worse, I said, "How about I receive it with gratitude on the day that you cross?"

It was remarkable—astonishing, really—that the camp was still being organized and managed by this small, rotating team of elected leaders. Remarkable, too, was the fact that after almost three months, there was still no large-scale mobilization of assistance for the roughly fifteen hundred people living in tent camps pressed up against the Juárez–El Paso border. I'd always felt this, but I had slowly grown used to it, at least until Tania Guerrero brought a group from the international human rights agency Human Rights Watch to the street.

They were astonished by the level of self-governance the community had established, and were clearly impressed with the leadership team and all they had accomplished. The community was orderly, law-abiding, cleaned up after themselves, and had never once caused a problem to any of the businesses around them, or to any of the passersby who walked through their homes all day and all night. They were impressed by the way the kids were cared for, too, both individually and as a whole, and also by the leaders' ability to keep the community both cohesive and fair. But they were shocked by the state of things on the street, as well as in the other two encampments in town.

The conditions were bad; of course, that was a given. But it was the lack of mobilization that really struck them. Where were the international agencies? they asked. And where was the infrastructure to help keep people safe? If this were going on at the edge of any other nation's border, there would be an outcry. If this were anywhere but at the foot of the United States, the United States themselves would be speechifying against it. This is what they said, not me, and it helped.

"Human Rights Watch: Tyranny Has a Witness" their caps and their tote bags proclaimed. And in that place and at that time, at least, it was true. A witness with clout. It made a real difference. To be honest, after just a few hours, a part of me wanted to run away with them like a kid to the circus. And why not? Their area of concern was the entire border; their field of expertise global migration, and there was something both bracing and deeply refreshing about their broad and coherent perspective. But they were humble too: generous and patient and curious, they spent as long as it took to listen and learn and try to understand.

With help from Víctor and Homero—who were as scrupulous as ever about matching people's IDs with the new fichas, and then with the names written out carefully in ink on pieces of paper attached to clipboards layered over with sheaths of plastic as protection from the rain—the team finally accompanied three families up to the checkpoint and helped eleven people to cross.

It took about two and a half minutes for them to do this—literally—which was both wonderful and enraging. Proof of the lie that "we have no space." And proof too that even the lowest level of Border Patrol officer knew the illegality of what they were doing.

Still, we all slept better that night knowing that the Human Rights Watch team would return again the next day. And when they did, helping another four families—seventeen people—to get through in less than ten minutes, it brought hope alive again. Víctor was at least as relieved as anyone on the street. His family had been number thirty-four before Human Rights Watch had come. Now they were number twenty-seven. And as he updated the list—starting over with a fresh sheet of paper for the umpteenth time and carefully writing out: (1) Juan Carlos Flores Marino (6), (2) Ramona Toledo Cruz (2), (3) Saul Escobedo Reyes (5)—he actually started singing to himself.

It was strange and also disturbing, then, to see Víctor and his family at the top of the bridge by the checkpoint the very next morning. He was sitting on the sidewalk close to the orange barrier, with his wife, Antonia, and their four young girls, and they were all packed up and ready to go. Taken aback, also worried, I climbed over the barrier separating the US-to-Mexico sidewalk from the street, wove my way through the traffic, and then scrambled over the barrier onto the Mexico-to-US side to greet them. I'd been trying to put my collar on as I crossed, and while I velcroed it together and tucked it under my sweatshirt, Víctor told me that some men had come to the camp the night before asking for "the one who runs the list."

There had been three of them, he said. Clearly threatening, obviously broadcasting their ability to harm, they stopped someone, who led them to someone else, who insisted that the family of the man who runs the list had gone to "an albergue, or a hotel, or who knew where for the night" . . . until finally the men left, warning they'd be back.

No one on the street knew the men or recognized them even, but everyone assumed they were looking for Víctor because of his refusal to sell spots on the list. Out of fear for his safety, the community voted unanimously to send them up to the bridge right away as a result.

This was the second time I'd heard of this happening. Weeks before, Gloria, a terrified, spectacled woman traveling alone with two children, had begun to feel threatened when heavily armed federal police started driving slowly down the street in their pickup trucks as if looking for someone. Her husband, from whom she was in flight, was a federale back in Guerrero. Had he told them to look for her? Had they seen she was here? Would he come now to take her away? Would they?

I'd been helping Juan Carlos to establish regular community meetings back then, and when Gloria asked for help, I suggested she petition the community at that afternoon's meeting, which she did. I had no idea how the community would respond. So many were in flight themselves, so many were terrified. Not wanting to influence things one way or another, I left the meeting before Gloria spoke, and only after it was all over did I learn that they voted unanimously for her to move up to number one on the list.

I was astonished by this magnanimity, I have to admit. When I expressed as much to one of the leaders he was genuinely shocked by my surprise. "But Cristi," he said. "We have to maintain our humanity!"

This, then, is how Víctor's family came to be at the top of the bridge that morning. He and his wife were visibly shaken, the result of fear both fresh and remembered, I think. And perhaps that fear leaped into me, I'm not sure. All I know is that I couldn't stand it. I mean literally. I tried to sit and wait and be and join, but I couldn't. A minute felt like an hour, ten minutes like a day, and before I'd even made it to twenty, I stood up, marched across to the barrier, and demanded to speak to a supervisor.

"You're free to go through—you're a citizen, right?" one of the officers said, noncommittal. So I charged back down the bridge to the Border Patrol offices on the US side. And then, for the first time ever, I demanded to speak to whomever was in charge.

It didn't take long for the shift supervisor to arrive. Tall, thin, and languid, he extended his hand to me as he approached and we greeted each other politely, he in his uniform and me in mine.

Nothing I said managed to snag his interest though. At one point he asked why I didn't advise "this leader" to leave Juárez for someplace else in Mexico if he was in so much danger. Later he recommended I speak to the Mexican government about getting him on their list. And even then I kept my cool. I am wearing a collar, I kept reminding myself; I am visibly a priest, which helped.

Finally, with a sigh, the supervisor pulled out a pen and then a miniature pad from his pocket and asked for Víctor's last name. "Okay, Reverend," he said, once I'd given it to him. "I'll see what I can do." Then he turned and walked away, leaving me, now just the tiniest bit hopeful, to walk back up to the checkpoint and wait.

And wait.

And wait.

And wait.

After three hours, two of the girls needed fresh diapers. A new leader named Joselin came up with a bag of them, along with as many blankets as she could carry. Later Homero came up to give his own jacket to Víctor, who'd insisted his wife and kids take the blankets and was shivering. One of the girls, the littlest one, drew shapes in a small green pad I'd found in the bottom of my bag. Sitting with her back against the orange barrier, she looked (again! what was it about these children?) like an executive of great power, sitting in her corner office, doing her work. Her mother and I exchanged silent smiles about this. Otherwise, the same, anxious nothing . . . and nothing . . . and nothing. . . .

At one point Víctor asked Antonia if she'd brought the huipil and she said yes, of course, and then brought the embroidered blouse out of her backpack and handed it to me. As gently as I could, I refused to take it, "Not quite yet," I said.

Later I looked for birds in the river below. Photographed them. Sat back down.

The shift changed, and when Víctor checked in with the new officers, one of them finally called down to the offices on her walkie-talkie. The previous supervisor had left for the day, she said, but he'd spoken with the "incoming supe," who was aware of the situation. There was no room right now, she told Víctor. Yes, we were welcome to wait. No, there was no way of telling when there might be space.

Back to hour after hour of nothing. To praying silently with rosaries Betty's friend, Sister Bea, had given me and I had given them; to watching the older girls play games on their father's phone; to the littlest one tracing shapes in the dust now on the orange barrier itself; to staring at the brass plaque that read Estado De Mexico, and then a line, and then United States of America.

Beside me, Antonia was growing increasingly rigid—with fear or with cold, I couldn't tell. I asked if there was a way I could help her relax into the waiting, and literally the second I spoke that last word—*waiting*—the female officer pointed to me and said, "Okay."

"Okay?" I repeated, stupidly.

"Yes. Okay," she said again, as nonchalant as can be. "They can come in."

And that was it. One by one, Víctor and Antonia and their four daughters rose to their feet, and one by one we kissed and hugged each other goodbye. Then, with a spluttering smile, I said to Víctor: "I'll take that huipil now if it's okay with you," and close to tears himself, he smiled shakily back as he gave it to me, folded, I thought, like a flag.

Then he turned, fell in line behind one of the officers, and led his family in silence past the orange barrier and into their chance at new lives.

24

No one through.

No one through.

No one through.

No one through.

25

EVERY NOW AND then it is good to step back and remember the basics. Any human being in flight for their lives is guaranteed the right, by both US and international law, to ask for the protection of a neighboring country. This has been the case in the United States since 1951, when we joined 145 other countries in signing the UN-backed charter that first outlined the rights—and international standards of treatment—of displaced people. Known as the "Convention Relating to the Status of Refugees," the charter sets out the rights of individuals who are granted asylum, the responsibilities of nations that grant asylum, and, most importantly, the universal right of all people in flight for their lives to request asylum of a neighboring country.

No one disputes any of this. It is simply a fact. And, at the same time, every single day at checkpoints and ports of entry up and down the border, the right to request asylum is denied hundreds—possibly thousands—of times. Our own government breaks our own laws every day, then. Knowingly. Intentionally. And repeatedly.

This breaking of our own laws should be no less shocking because it is frequent and flagrant than it would be if it were occasional and hidden. Lack of shame should not equal lack of blame.

But, somehow, it does. It is under the cover of all this flagrant visibility, in fact, that our immigration process has devolved into a series of knotted, legal dead ends, which undermine and ultimately circumvent that which it was established to uphold in the first place.

This dismantling of our nation's asylum system has been intentional, that's the thing: the result of an evolving, calculated, step-by-step take-down of the protections we were—and are—legally obliged to offer. As one administration official put it in a leaked memo to colleagues back in July 2019, "My mantra has persistently been presenting aliens with multiple, unsolvable dilemmas." To this end, hundreds of protocols, large and small, were enacted in order to ensnare, confound, and ultimately deter thousands of applicants from effectively pursuing their asylum claims. And when a particular group of people found a way around one, another would be dreamed up, and then quickly implemented, in order to block their progress.

It was when a woman named Paulina and her five children were returned to the street that we first started to hear about the newest of these policies: HARP. Yet another acronym for yet another previously unthinkable protocol, the Humanitarian Asylum Review Process was launched as a pilot program in El Paso just a couple of weeks earlier. HARP fast-tracked the asylum process, flipping it into hyperdrive and reducing the hearing process from years to just days, allowing a final determination to be declared within the four walls of an immigration detention center right there on the border.

This caused all kinds of problems—impossibilities, really—for asylum seekers, not the least of which was the profound unlikelihood of being able to secure legal representation while being locked in a detention facility with only one guaranteed phone call a month.

The most radical and alarming aspect of HARP, however, was the fact that the all-important credible fear interviews were now to be given by Border Patrol officers, instead of by specially trained asylum review experts. This reversed decades of established practice in which asylum review officers were well trained *and* assiduously protected from political pressure in order to uphold the integrity of the interviews themselves. This sudden switch in personnel led legal experts and human rights advocates to conclude that credible fear interviews were no longer being used to sort credible applications for asylum from incredible ones. Instead, it seemed, credible fear interviews were now being used as an initial, insurmountable hurdle to entering the process in the first place.

As far as any of us could tell, Paulina and her children were the first people from the community to have their request for asylum permanently denied under these brand-new auspices. After years of terrified and locked-down life under the warring cartels in Michoacán, months of living on the street, six days of being number one on the list, and then ten days in US detention, Paulina learned that her request for asylum had finally—and permanently—been denied. There were no lawyers, and there was no judge, and Paulina had very little idea about what had happened at all, or what it meant, beyond the absolute fact that her hopes for a new life in safety had been shattered.

When word got out about what had happened, the community gathered around Paulina and her kids on the corner of the street closest to the bridge. She was trying desperately not to cry. The kids were blank. Stone-faced. Unnaturally still. Between them, they now owned a transparent bag filled with individual packs of saltine crackers and a purple plastic folder full of paperwork.

The two oldest boys had been separated from the rest of the family as soon as they'd entered the system, and all I could think to do was get them a hotel room for the night so they could at least be together, and have a shower, and get some sleep in a safe place. But as we prepared to leave, Martín walked into our path, stopping us.

Stretching out his hand, Martín offered Paulina pretty much all he had left in the way of money: a fifty-peso bill and a couple of twenties. "Take it, please," he said. "I'm sorry I don't have more."

Others followed. One by one people processed forward, as solemnly as if they were in church during Holy Week, and silently gave what they had to this now lost and despairing mother of five. And with the most profound dignity imaginable, she received it all: the love, the support, the money, silently nodding her thanks as she blinked back tears.

"What will you do now?" I asked as we walked to the hotel.

"Go back home," she said. "What else can I do?"

"Will you be safe there?"

"No," she said flatly, entirely matter of fact. "First my oldest boy, then my next, and one day the little one, too, will have to choose: join the cartel or be shot."

If things were bad before—oppressively random, and illegally delayed, and hot in the day, and cold at night, and exposed twenty-four hours a day to whatever happened out on the street in the heart of one of the most dangerous cities on earth—they became worse after Paulina and her children were returned. At the time, none of us could understand how an asylum claim could be both initiated *and* concluded in just a few days. It wasn't until later—when we called the team from Human Rights Watch, who told us they'd heard rumors about this new protocol, HARP—that we began to understand, and I found myself again seething with grief and rage that felt too big to hold.

Walking back across the bridge that evening, I brushed past the officers at the checkpoint, scowled as rudely as I could, and refused to respond to one of the officers' wishes that I "have a good evening." It was so easy to do this—to alleviate my own sense of powerlessness by blaming the men and women of Border Patrol, and I'm sorry to say that I did it often. The truth is, of course, that most of them were just doing their job. Tell them to let everyone in, and they'd let everyone in. Tell them to kick everyone out, and they'd kick everyone out. Like most of us, many officers cared more about overtime, and mortgage payments, and their kids' Little League games than they did about immigration policy. Some did seem to enjoy the power they wielded, and a few clearly reveled in it. But others were visibly disturbed by the ways they were being asked to act, the things they were being asked to do.

A couple of months earlier, for example, Cristina Coronado's friend Sigrid and I had a brief, impromptu meeting with a shift supervisor who did his best to answer our questions. He started by trotting out the official line. "We never deny anyone the chance to apply for asylum. That would be illegal," he said. "We just tell them we don't have room—" But then he seemed to lose the conviction he was going to need to complete the thought and interrupted himself. "Ach! It's really just a question of semantics, I guess," he said, looking down to the ground, scuffing his shoes.

It is only true to say, too, that I'd seen several officers act with kindness and care up at the checkpoint. I'm not going to use their names. The last thing I want to do is cause them any trouble. But I saw officers hand their own sweaters to shivering children, and their gloves, and even their lunch, carefully packed back at home in blue-lidded Tupperware. Once a ten-year-old boy—the middle child of a family of seven—told me that an officer leaned over the checkpoint's orange barricade, fixed his eyes on the boy's, and said, in Spanish, "I was you once," before starting to cry.

I didn't see this myself, but it was easy to believe because the very next evening, while I waited to have my own passport checked, this same officer recognized me and beckoned me to him, insisting I jump the line.

"Did they get through?" he asked, leaning out across the barrier designed to keep him separate from me when I approached, keen as a kid himself. And when I replied, "No. Not yet," he sank back onto his stool again, deflated and confused.

All of which is to say clearly, again, that it's too easy to blame Border Patrol. It is true that it is their job to implement policies along the border, but it is not uniquely theirs. Policies implemented by our government are made on behalf of us all—which means, in a very real way, that we are all implicated by and responsible for what goes on there.

As I again tried to sleep that night, safe in my bed in my little pink room, all I could see was Paulina carrying that fluttery pile of money like a baby bird in the cupped palm of her hand all the way to the hotel. She was Jesus on the way to the cross, I knew. She really was Jesus on the way to the cross.

And who does that make me? I wondered all night. And who does it make all of us on this side of the border? I mean, if Paulina and Víctor and Martín and all the others who are giving what they have for the sake of another are standing in the place of Jesus, as they so visibly and indisputably are, where is it, exactly, that the rest of us are standing?

26

THANKSGIVING DAY, AND Skinny María was dead. She'd passed away three days earlier, but it was only now that her partner let me know. I hadn't realized, at first, that they were a couple: frail, homeless Jesús, with the bad back and the miniature tent in front of the bus stop, who'd begged his way into the community and swept both sides of the sidewalk up and down the block every day since, and scarily thin María, who clearly struggled with addiction and dressed up every night in too-bright makeup and too-tight clothes so that it was clear what she did for a living. María, who asked me for painkillers almost every time I saw her. María, who when she didn't ask for painkillers, which I never gave her, asked instead for money or for food, which I did—which in turn prompted occasional grouchy speeches from the generous and long-suffering asylum seekers who did their best to support even this feckless couple (Didn't I know what she would do with the money? Didn't I know how she would spend it?). Skinny María with the glowing eyes, always brimming, and the cheekbones so sharp a part of me always wanted to flee. María, who the community sometimes, heartbreakingly, called La Mala, had died. She had gotten a cold in the wet and the rain of the week before, Jesús said. He'd managed to persuade her to go to the hospital, but her lungs were already too infected, and she, well, she, then she just . . . "passed away."

I was standing in the middle of the street when Jesús told me this. I'd finished the day's class and then met with the latest couple who seemed to have been returned under HARP: Raquel and her husband, Gilberto, who were distraught—utterly rattled and weeping—after being turned down for asylum through a process they didn't understand. Yes, they were given some papers, they told me impatiently when I asked. And yes, they were interviewed—twice, Gilberto said.

But what he really wanted me to know was that their daughter, the younger one, Ana, who had Down syndrome, had been repeatedly shouted at "in there" and once even shoved as if she were a criminal, he said—"or as if she weren't human at all." We called Tania Guerrero and made a plan to meet the following day. Then I'd finally begun to leave, already late for Thanksgiving dinner with Peter and Betty.

Only that's when Jesús approached, fiddling shyly with the lapel of his jacket, saying, "Es que María, mi flaquita, mi María flaquita ha fallecido." He didn't want a service, and he didn't want a prayer. He just wanted me to know because he knew I cared for her, he said. Everyone else in the community treated them badly, speaking rudely to them and throwing their things away—"Even my tent," he said then. "Look. Gone. All gone." And it was true. His miniature tent was indeed gone.

"Where do you sleep?" I asked, stupidly. And he shrugged as he said with something that sounded like shame, "On the sidewalk."

But the thing is, he said then, he was wondering if he could have a little money so he could send something to his mother-in-law to help cover the costs of the funeral. And while this gave me hope—he was still thinking, still playing the angles—I told him I didn't have any money to give. This lie made me feel cold and hollow inside, and all through the moving Thanksgiving feast at Peter and Betty's, I couldn't shake the notion that I was in the wrong place: inside, even with these extraordinary people, instead of outside with Jesús, and with the spirity presence of María, and with the shaken, scared, regretful, weepy presence of Raquel and Gilberto as they tried to make sense of these latest traumatizing experiences.

Lest that sound pure, though, or good, or even kind, I need to record here that I hurried past the street when I walked back to the bridge later that afternoon, hoping no one would see me. And that I was, once again, hugely and shamefully grateful to be back in the muted, safe-beyond-imagining streets of El Paso that evening and then in the pink room of the little yellow house, alone, with the door closed.

Here are excerpts from the records of Raquel and Gilberto's credible fear interviews—the opportunity for which they'd lived out on the sidewalk, with two children, for more than two months.

First Raquel:

> Why are you here today?
> *Because I saw on Facebook to come here and request help to get into the US and I brought my kids with me to make it quicker to come into the US.*
> Why didn't you apply for a visa?
> *Because I did not qualify.*

> Were you harmed?
> *No.*
> Did you file a police report?
> *No.*
> Did someone advise you to come seek help or asylum?
> *Yes. We read it on the internet. On Facebook. It said to come to America and they would let us in.*
> What are your intentions in the United States?
> *I want to go live with my sister and work.*
> Do you plan to return to your home country?
> *Yes.*

And Gilberto:

> Do you fear going back to your home country?
> *No.*
> Why are you here today?
> *I want to request asylum so I can work.*
> Why are you requesting asylum?
> *Because I want a better life for my family.*
> Do you know what asylum is?
> *No.*

Any one of these answers would have led Raquel and Gilberto's asylum application to be denied even in the days before HARP because, with them, the couple made it clear they had neither a case nor any idea what asylum meant. Now, though, HARP had reduced credible fear interviews from a gateway into the system to a locked and almost insurmountable barrier for those with even the most urgent need for protection. In response, Human Rights Watch and the American Civil Liberties Union (ACLU) were planning to bring a lawsuit against the government in the name of those rejected and returned under its auspices. People would likely die because of HARP. People we knew. This was a fact. And, at the same time, Raquel and Gilberto's return reminded us that not everyone on the street had anything like a valid claim to the particular protections of asylum. Nothing is ever as simple as we want it to be. Nothing is as black or as white. Instead, the presence of multiple, simultaneous, and seemingly contradictory realities makes something more like a storm-cloud gray: various, and layered, and ever-shifting—and urgent, nonetheless.

Again: the violence besetting Michoacán and Zacatecas and Guerrero was real, pervasive, and appalling. People—I mean taxi drivers and marketplace vendors and woodcutters and fishermen and farmers and teachers and corner-store owners—were routinely extorted, frequently kidnapped, and often then tortured before being killed. Most of the time there was no counterforce—no state, or set of laws, or police force, or militia—to oppose any of this. Which meant that when someone demands more than you make every week for "protection," or when your husband or child is kidnapped, or even when your entire family is murdered, there is nowhere to turn and no one to turn to.

There is a careful performance of a different reality, of course. Cops arrive with wailing sirens and flashing lights, photos are taken, interviews recorded and transcribed. But in the end, as you have always known, impunity wins the day. If you are stronger, you win. If you are weaker, and you don't do what your stronger neighbor decrees, well, you lose: entirely and absolutely, every time.

This is how it was for most people at the foot of the bridge. Whole families fled to the border in acute fear for their lives, or because "they"—this was always the subject of the sentence; nothing else, just "they"—had already murdered someone in the family: a son, a husband, a brother, a sister. These people were terrified, and grief-stricken, and deeply traumatized—and nonetheless remained steadfastly determined to keep themselves and the rest of their families alive. Which meant applying for asylum in the United States. Which meant hope.

But this was also true: some people were crammed with their children up against the border in flimsy tents because while the violence had not yet touched them personally, they also wanted out. They wanted to be able to work, of course, but also to live a life with at least a little security. By which I mean to be able to work without giving almost all they earned to armed thugs or to send their kids to school without worrying all day whether they would be kidnapped. Many in this group did not have an officially viable asylum claim. Some had no idea what the term even meant. Like Gilberto and Raquel, they'd come to the border because someone on Facebook (a friend? a family member? a coyote focusing on poor Mexicans because his trade in Central Americans had dried up?) had told them that, if they approached now, America would let them in. It was finally their turn, they were told—but hurry! The window would close on November 30, or December 10, or January 3.

Some people, in other words, had come to the border not because they were specifically threatened or physically harmed by the cartels and the system that both enabled and empowered them but because they were tricked, or lied to, or told broken-to-smithereens half-truths, which isn't great either.

Both groups were victims then—those with genuine asylum claims and those without—because both were bit players in a game over which they had zero control. They were, every one of them, people without power: exposed, deeply vulnerable, proud, and, in the eyes of the world (God forgive us), disposable.

And there was also this. There was a new family: delicate mother with a newborn so thoroughly wrapped in green I never saw its face; sharp-cheeked father, young, hopped up, hugely intense; and their eight-year-old daughter, who looked just like her dad and shouted out answers in class at an entirely different pace from the others and with a searing intensity that at first made me laugh and then made me nervous. This family, who had been on the street for just two days, was already at number one on the list. How did this happen?

Money, I thought first. But like Víctor before him, Homero was passionately anticorruption, and the ficha system seemed to be working. So what then—violence? Or threats of violence, at least? I will never know for sure. But he scared me, the dad. Truly. His very presence was menacing.

Everyone was there on the street by then, in other words: legitimate asylum seekers, economic migrants, even some of those responsible for the horror in the first place. And how could it really be otherwise? Victims and bystanders and victimizers and local street people all living hugger-mugger in the tents and lean-tos up and down the street, meeting and going to class and fetching water and cleaning the street together, hour after hour after hour, as I sort of bumbled around, doing my best in my own clunky way to embrace and be embraced by them all. But the depth of my simplicity was being ever more deeply exposed; my simplicity and my thin, blinkered, US-style privilege, which allowed me to believe that if *this* was true, it necessarily followed that *that* was not.

But all of it was true. And all of it was true at the very same time. Sandra was right: reality was layered like an onion, and every layer made you cry.

27

No one through. One family returned.

No one through.

No one through. Another family returned.

28

HIS FOURTH DAY on the street, the terrifying man walked right up to me in the middle of class and asked in that way that isn't really a question if I'd accompany his family, right then, up to the top of the bridge. Genuinely astonished, I said I was in the middle of class and busy with the children, which sent him back to the bench at the edge of the room, where he sat, arms crossed and staring, for the rest of the class. The moment we were finished, though, even as kids were still getting in line, he, his wife with the baby, and their daughter approached me again, all backpacked up and ready to go.

Once more the father stood too close, and once more he asked me to go with them to the checkpoint. Only this time there was no hint of a question mark in his voice. "Not just yet," I said skittishly, angered and then afraid again—a single, shining thread of fear though, not unmanageable. "I need to get the kids back to the street. But after that, and if the leaders approve, then yes," I said—feeling like a coyote, like a pawn. "I will accompany you to the bridge."

And I did.

We checked in first with Homero and others, who shamefacedly affirmed that the new family was now number one on the list, then summoned the families now legitimately at numbers two and three. When everyone had gathered, we set off for the turnstiles full of unexpressed shame, fear and anger, and without even a cursory prayer.

Less than two hours later, they all got through, and though it is terrible to admit, the main thing I felt then was relief. Not joy. Not gratitude. Not even peace. Only a bitter kind of strained exhale: the terrifying man wouldn't be around anymore.

I didn't sleep at all that night. Swamped by retroactive fear far deeper than I had allowed myself to feel at the time, I didn't know even how to pray it through. Peter. John. All the Marys. The ambitious sons of Zebedee. Even Judas. They were all there too—weren't they?—out on the streets in community together, duplicitous and loyal, compromised and faithful, and all of them essential in their own conflicting ways. But it felt as if I was losing my bearings and toppling in. I felt infected almost. Complicit. And for the first time in a long time, I wanted to run away.

It got so bad it made me nauseous. I called an old friend in Mexico City, someone I'd known well for years and loved, and to him I was able to jabber out a waterfall of words that at least expressed my vertigo. Then I called my journalist friend Sandra, and when we met later for supper, I told her what had happened.

"Oh no. This is not good, Tina," she said. "I am so sorry. This is . . . well, I don't want to say anything terrible, but this is very dangerous. It means that one day they may come up and say"—here she pressed the points of two fingers into my ribs like the nozzle of a gun—"'Take me up the bridge now.'" And for just a second, her fingers became a real gun. And I froze.

"You cannot go on this way," Sandra said then, as if she knew. And she did know. She'd been a journalist for more than ten years in a city where just being a journalist was life-threatening.

In 2008, a friend of hers who had been reporting on the shadowy but real connections between the cartels, the police, and the local government had been shot dead in his car as he was taking his daughter to school. And in 2010, a second reporter from her paper, a photographer this time, had also been murdered as a result of his work.

I was completely in awe of Sandra's courage and integrity. I'd met her soon after I arrived in Juárez, and the first night we'd met, as she drove me back to the bridge after a long, late dinner, I'd asked how she dared live her life the way she did. "It's very simple, Tina," she'd said. "The only reason I am alive is because no one has decided to kill me. Until they do, I will be fine, and the moment they do, I will be dead. There is no point worrying."

Courage like this both bolstered and shamed me now. There I was, undone at the first hint of threat, when all around me people were contending with levels of real danger I couldn't even fully imagine. It wasn't only Sandra, of course. So many on the street were there because of real and appalling threats to their safety. Just a few days earlier, a woman named Yuritzi had sat down next to me on the curb, and when I asked how she was, she said, "Not angry today, more . . . I think . . . sad." I'd settled in and done my best to make room for whatever she was feeling while her toddler ran in and out of her lap. The little boy, too young for class, tripped over her feet at one point, and when he started to cry, she gave him a large brown nut to suck on. This soothed him. The process of trying to crack the hard shell with his teeth kept him happy, for a bit. But then he saw his dad, pushed himself up out of her lap again, and ran down the street, yelling "Papi, Papi, help me open this nut?" and that was when Yuritzi had sighed and started to cry.

"They dumped a dead body, chopped into chunks, in a garbage bag in front of our house," she said. "And because it was outside of our house, people thought we were somehow to blame. For this reason, we went nowhere near it. Drew the drapes and closed our eyes and stayed in the house like we weren't there. Can you imagine this? A dead human body, chopped into chunks and falling out of the bag, right there in front of your house?

"After a time, dogs started tugging, pulling at bits, dragging them away to eat until, finally, the police did come. Then they did as we knew they would: they knocked on our door and asked us why we thought the body was dropped there, in front of our home. That was the night that we left."

The truth was that I couldn't imagine this happening in front of my home. Not really. But its reality in Yuritzi's life settled into me nonetheless. I took it back to my room and wrote it out on a small yellow note card, which I placed on my altar, along with all the other note cards covered with stories of horror and death that were already there. Then I lit a candle and sat, still and silent, in front of it, hoping that somehow this did something to alleviate Yuritzi's suffering. Now, though, I'd been snagged myself by just the tiniest corner of violence and threat. And rather than abate my fear, the gathered truths of others instead seemed to augment it.

Sandra removed her fingers from my side and ordered another round of drinks. "In my opinion, you have two options," she said. "I think you won't like the first one, but it would be the best: you stop going to the street completely. At least for a time."

I said I couldn't do that. I had to teach class each day, at the very least. "Okay, then you must stop being predictable," she said firmly. "Stop being reliable. Stop arriving at the same time and leaving at the same time. Stop being the person who goes up to the checkpoint every day, no matter what."

Back home, I was troubled by these last words in particular. I was able to do so little, and almost all of it rested on my doing what I said I would do, when I said I would do it. Even the idea—that I would now become someone whose actions were as arbitrary and unreliable as everything else on the border—felt sickening.

Add to this the fact that families were by then being regularly returned under HARP, which was even further eroding and effectively running an endgame around even the most grounded and evidence-filled requests for asylum, and the subsequent presence on the street of lawyers from the ACLU who required photographs of paperwork and signed forms for their lawsuit, and I found myself getting more and more tangled in the constant, divergent strands of need and urgency and fear. And then: panic, like a whisk in the brain, mixing thoughts too quickly until they ran together like a blurred train passing, which, again, birthed the desire to flee—to match speed with speed and simply get out of there.

What was essential was to find a way to remain. And in order to do that—to remain in at least relative safety—there needed to be both a diminishment of whatever minuscule power I'd accrued on the bridge and also a sharing of it. What I needed, Sandra helped me see, was some kind of external stay, which limited my ability to go up to the bridge and which made it clear that doing so was reliant on something more regulated and absolute than my own desire. The point wasn't to flee from whatever power I had then, but to find the best way to continue to use it. I called friends back in Boston, and mentors, and then, finally, I called Canon Lee and together we figured it out.

There would be a new policy: a diocesan directive, which prohibited priests from accompanying people to the checkpoint alone. From then on, a minimum of two ordained members of the clergy would be required. Better three.

At the community meeting the following day, I told everyone about the new directive, explaining that there now needed to be at least two priests to go up to the checkpoint and that therefore my accompaniment of folks to the bridge would stop being so regular. It was out of my hands, I said, looking at the ground. And in part because everyone in the community was used to the way power wielded at a distance filtered into their lives through changes like this, not one single person asked me why the change had been made so suddenly. Instead, their responses were muted and accepting on the surface and (rightly) suspicious underneath. "I've heard you are not going to be helping us anymore, Maestra," a newly arrived father said after class that day, and I couldn't tell if I felt afraid, or ashamed, when he did.

Homero and I never spoke a word to each other about any of this. It must have been at least partly in response to the sharp-cheeked man's too-quick rise through the list, though, that he designed a new, improved ficha for the community. Still based on Víctor's original, each card was now also marked by his own specially designed *Puente Paso del Norte* stamp bought with funds from the communal kitty.

Homero spent hours painstakingly inking, stamping, and numbering each card himself and then writing the names of adults and the number of children in each family before signing and sealing each one with sticky-backed plastic. I spent a fair amount of time that week sitting quietly with him on the sidewalk, helping to peel and then stick down the plastic. And as I did, I couldn't help wondering: What did the sharp-cheeked man threaten him with to move so fast to the top of the list? What did he say, specifically? Or did he say nothing at all? Did he just approach too fast, and stand too close, and stare too hard, and ask his questions with the kind of flat finality that made them demands, the way he had done with me?

Homero had been victimized and targeted the way so many on the street had been victimized and targeted. His asylum case, he'd been told, was "strong." All I knew of his life before was that he'd been a peanut seller and the proud owner of his own cart—which he had lost forever now, no matter what happened at the border. Homero's leadership style on the street, though, was both firm and gentle, which made me think he'd led groups of people before—people who were fighting against the odds.

It was both poignant and a real honor, then, to accompany him, his wife, and his child up to the checkpoint with another priest, Sarah, a week or so later. I'll never know the details of his case, but they must have been both extreme and terrible because his family was one of the very, very few to make it all the way through the system back then, despite the steep hurdle of HARP. Or perhaps it was just luck. Or some kind of quota that needed to be maintained in order to at least look like the system was functioning. Who knows?

29

I'M NOT SURE if this is correct or not, but it seemed possible that getting through the checkpoint began to get easier after the terrifying, sharp-cheeked man and then Homero and his family got through. I went up with Lee. I went up with Sara. I even went up with a woman in training to become a deacon who Lee let wear a collar for the task. And at least every two or three days, a small group of families got through. Of course, families were being returned by HARP more regularly by then, too, and it was entirely possible that these two facts were linked. Did this less reluctant access to the asylum process signify a policy shift? And if so, was it one toward or against Mexican asylum seekers? Could it be that Border Patrol was letting folks in only because they had a new way to kick them back out again under HARP? It was possible. Perhaps even likely.

What was certain was that more and more families were being returned under HARP each day, which meant that, among adults at least, fear continued to rise, along with exhaustion and despair. And what a terrible, inverted trinity that is: fear, exhaustion, and despair.

Every day families walked back across the bridge into Juárez, recognizable to everyone as returnees because of the detention center gray sweatshirts or sweatpants they wore, and the color-coded paper bracelets, and the transparent envelopes filled with papers very few of them understood. And even beyond the individual hopelessness their return induced in the utterly exhausted returnees themselves (What now? Where now? How now?), the impact of each returned family collided like a sledgehammer against the hope of the rest. For a minute you could practically see it: the echoing, one-by-one crumple as hope shattered, like some delicate thing dropped, every time a returned family turned left off the bridge and entered the street. The antidote for this used to be blaming the "failed" families themselves, but even this was now harder to sustain. Too many were being sent back: families with many children and grandparents with none; active, robust families; reluctant, shy families; and families with even the most terrifying stories of multiple disappearances and deaths too brutal and gruesome to fully absorb.

By the middle of December, it seemed to be dawning on people up and down the street—people who had been there for months and people who had only just arrived—that the US system was once again having its way. HARP was closing the window the Mexicans had found, and there was less and less chance of getting into the States for anyone at all.

Even on a day when families did manage to get through the checkpoint, then, there was little joy. Too many were being returned for people to convince themselves that getting through meant much of anything anymore. But it was why we were all there, so on we went, going through the motions, hoping against hope that first this and then that family would beat the odds and manage not only to get in but also to stay.

Few new families were arriving on the street anymore, and there was more room on the sidewalks for those who did. A green tent next to the water table was now filled with piles of folded tarps and mattresses and blankets belonging to people long gone.

And Yuritzi, now one of the community leaders herself, was able to give every new family more than they needed to get settled in.

I was spending an increasing percentage of my time making trips to a small basement office in the government building just a couple of blocks from the street, where bus tickets for Mexican asylum seekers who'd been returned from the States were being subsidized by as much as 50 percent. Even with this generous subsidy, though, it still cost about $450 for a family of five to travel from Juárez to Michoacán by bus. $450. That's more than an average month's wage.

The despair that shrouded the returned families was both palpable and brutalizing, and they moved on quickly. Only one mother with her single child returned to the street for the night. The rest slipped away from Juárez almost immediately. Some returned home, broke, deeply in debt, exhausted, and hopeless. Others could never return home as the danger was too real for them there, too pressing, and these set out for neighboring states, where the uncle of their cousin's wife lived, or the father of their daughter-in-law's best friend, in the hopes of having a place to stay at least and connections that might lead to work.

It was devastating.

But still people continued to try. Gerardo, Yuritzi, and Alejandro's father, Otilio, painstakingly updated the list every day and checked everyone's fichas before each approach. At least twice a week I'd accompanied a group of families, along with another priest, up to the checkpoint—which still sometimes worked and still sometimes didn't. And if all this wasn't enough, it was becoming clear by then, too, just how deeply the officers on the bridge were losing patience with my ongoing presence there.

One Thursday in mid-December, a visiting priest and I accompanied a group of three families to the checkpoint. There, as always, the heads of each family identified themselves as Mexican and then asked for asylum. The officers said there was no room. We waited, and they eventually radioed down to the Border Patrol offices at the base of the US side of the bridge. But instead of settling into hours of nothingness then, six officers came barreling up to the checkpoint like a wartime platoon and demanded to speak to me. What was my full legal name? they wanted to know. And what was my denomination? And was there someone in charge? A bishop? What was his name?

The answers to all these questions their leader furiously wrote down in a notebook, and I remembered Chief Gonzalez doing the same thing months before and wondered at the difference between me then and me now. Back in the early days, this sort of thing still felt important. Now it felt more like pantomime. The real power, I'd learned, lay not with these inflated and irate officers on the bridge but with suited policymakers in well-appointed rooms far away, rooms the officers had little more chance of entering than I did, rooms where programs like Zero Tolerance and MPP and HARP were meticulously and clinically constructed, step by lethal step.

"Evil is real," I wrote in my notebook that night. "But often—maybe mostly—it is polite too. And rational. And well-dressed. And well-educated."

I was finding it increasingly hard to go on—or even to get up in the morning. I'd make coffee, then read the portion of Scripture allotted for the day, and try to pray, and write a few notes in my journal, all from my bed in the little pink room. If it weren't for the kids, I'm not sure I'd have been able to keep going back to Juárez at all. They still had so much resilience, that's the thing. So much passion. So much desire. And their ability to metabolize horror into life force, day after day after day, felt literally miraculous.

One morning, for example, when it was pouring rain and everyone was hunkered down in their tents doing their best to keep dry, two young girls, both seven years old, charged up and down the street playing tag, laughing deliriously with the pleasure of getting so wantonly drenched. That very same day Alejandro read an entire book on iguanas out loud to the class, his whole being focused on the stuttering movement of his bent-tipped finger along the lines, as if we were all living the kind of lives where knowledge of an iguana's food preferences was the only thing we really needed. When he returned to his place on the bench by the table closest to the library, I noticed that the shark-obsessed twins, Miguel and Manuel, were again making what I later found out was a hammerhead out of rolled-up pieces of paper and tape. They did this no matter what the class project was, reimagining any assignment—to make cars out of geometric shapes or dream catchers out of tangled string—into the opportunity to make sharks.

They did this day after day, week after week, and always with the same glimmering and determined mischievousness: 3D plasticine sharks with fins and gills, abstract collages of large groups of sharks in the deep, and freestyle images they drew over and over and over again when the rest of the kids were drawing trees and flowers and houses and puppies. One day when we were learning about differences—big and small, hot and cold, wet and dry—Miguel and Manuel drew, colored, cut out, taped, and finally beamingly presented me with an image I've long thought should be on the cover of this little book: a great white shark, all giant jaws and murderous teeth lunging toward a skinny brown mouse person with big ears, and wide eyes, and arms raised in fear—or protest, or possibly even defeat.

30

Two families through. Three families returned.

No one through. One man returned.

Two families through. Four families returned.

One family through.

31

CELEBRATION IS IMPORTANT. *Celebration is important.* The idea felt impossible, also maybe grotesque, but I repeated it silently to myself over and over again anyway. Because even when everything was as dark and hopeless and full of fear and grief as it was each day in the second half of December—perhaps especially when everything was as dark and hopeless and full of fear and grief as it was each day in the second half of December—I knew that celebration really was important.

It was another of the truths the folks back in Boston had taught me, and it had been my mantra ever since the community first started to form by the Paso del Norte bridge. Back in early November, we'd created a beautiful celebration for the Day of the Dead. The community had hauled their way out of despair with the help of a rising altar made of fruit crates draped in white cloth and then gorgeously decorated, and paths strewn with marigold petals, and song, and prayer of the kind that sears even as it releases. Later, Sigrid and Tania had brought sweet pastries and a vat of hot coffee from the tent, and two teenage boys began to play norteño tunes on guitars we'd borrowed for the night. They'd played with real genius, strumming both together and apart, and singing melodies so piercing and at the same time so heavy with grief that I didn't think I'd be able to absorb any more. Then their father joined them, adding, with his voice, that slanted, rich tone full of longing that norteño also requires.

And everything and everyone fell silent then except the three of them, the youngest boy with his hoodie drooped down past his nose, the epitome of cool, and the older brother and the father, expressing all that could never be said with their song.

An hour later, the mood shifted again as the entire community gathered around the musicians with sodas and beers and—mostly because I am a priest and no one wants a priest at a party once it gets going—I headed back across the bridge to El Paso, singing myself, a little made-up ditty with only one line: thank you, Jesus, thank you / thank you, Jesus, thank you.

That had been earlier, though, back before HARP, when people still believed there was a chance of getting through to the States—and staying there. Now things were worse in just about every way, and it felt insane to even try to celebrate anything. But it was late December by then, almost Christmas, and at a time when everyone people knew were celebrating, some kind of celebration was required. A church back in Boston had collected money for gifts, and a group of mothers on the street had already made a list with the names and ages of every kid in the community. Then they had set off for the market at the other end of downtown, where they'd bought cheap (but pink!) digital mermaid watches, and soccer balls, and teething toys, and chunky plastic cars with soft wheels. Gifts alone, though, weren't enough to make a real celebration. So when Canon Lee and Bishop Michael suggested holding a posada on the street, I met with the leadership team, and together we chased back our wary exhaustion and said yes—yes, thank you, that would be great.

A posada is a traditional Mexican liturgy that commemorates the Holy Family's search for shelter in Bethlehem just before Jesus's birth. Walking in the proverbial steps of Mary and

Joseph, parish members make their way through their neighborhood, stopping at homes where lodging is refused, and refused, and then refused again—until, eventually, they find welcome somewhere, at which point they celebrate with food and drink and, these days at least, a piñata for the kids.

Canon Lee had reworked the posada especially for the community, paring it down so it would fit on one block. One day after class and a longer-than-usual community meeting, he and the bishop arrived on the street with a guitar, a bunch of booklets for the service, and a red Radio Flyer wagon filled with forty-five extra-large pizzas. Bishop Michael had asked if he should "dress up" for the occasion, and I'd said absolutely, all the way! So he arrived in purple, from head to toe: full-length purple cassock, wide purple cummerbund, even a purple skull cap. Lee was dressed as he always was, in a rumpled pair of a jeans and beat-up tweed jacket. He had his guitar and a couple of tiny Mary and Joseph costumes also, which two of the little ones put on, classically and adorably askew, as families gathered together in a growing huddle on the corner, waiting to be blessed by the bishop before the service began.

When we were ready, the entire community processed together from the corner closest to the bridge to the ice cream store a couple of hundred feet down the block. There we stopped and began to sing the song that has been sung at posadas for centuries. Here's a (slightly florid) English translation:

The Holy Family:

> *Pray give us lodging, dear sir, in the name of heav'n.*
> *All day since morning to travel we've giv'n.*

> *Mary, my wife, is expecting a child.*
> *She must have shelter tonight.*
> *Let us in, let us in!*

And here is the gatekeeper's reply:

> *You cannot stop here, I won't make my house*
> *an inn.*
> *I do not trust you, your story is thin.*
> *You two might rob me and then run away.*
> *Find somewhere else you can stay.*
> *Go away, go away!*

We moved on then, down past the bus stop, to the place where the sidewalk widened and we used to have class. The kids were starting to get into it, hustling toward a streetlamp, or a tightly stretched tarp, or whatever they could find to knock and knock on, giggling together as they went. The familiar feel of the liturgy even seemed to draw some of the parents back into memories they could ponder without too much stress or fear. But the collision between life on the street right then in Juárez and life on the street thousands of years ago in Bethlehem was giving me a kind of concussion. And as we continued to make our way down the block, asking to come in and being denied, asking to come in and being denied, it felt harder and harder to continue. Instead of joy, or comfort, or even a poignant kind of sorrow, I felt only rage. The story was so old. So foundational. And so precisely enacted there every day. It was too real, perhaps. Too much.

Here is verse two:
Holy Family

> *Please show us pity, your heart can't be so hard.*
> *Look at poor Mary, so worn and so tired.*
> *We are most poor, but we'll pay what we can.*
> *God will reward you, good man.*
> *Let us in, let us in!*

And the gatekeeper:

> *You try my patience. I'm tired and must get some rest.*
> *I've told you nicely, but still you insist.*
> *If you don't go and stop bothering me,*
> *I'll fix you, I guarantee.*
> *Go away, go away!*

What else is there to say? I thought. And what else is there to do? That self-proclaimed Christians in the United States supported our policies at the border made a mockery of the story of the birth of Jesus himself, and was simply grotesque. There was no theological stance—none, I thought—that could possibly uphold or excuse this position. I knew I was being extreme, and sounded didactic even to myself. But it was true, I countered, and then silently insisted, and sometimes it was important to be clear: supporting our nation's immigration policies while claiming to be a Christian is a fiction and a lie. This is the thought I was filled with that night, and I still think it is true; it is, quite simply, impossible.

Back on the street, my queasiness was neither dispersed nor diluted by the extravagant pizza fest we held at the end of the posada, to at least symbolize welcome and safety and relief. About forty-five minutes after we finished, the bishop, Lee, a wonderful volunteer named Doug, and I left the remaining pizzas with the community and went up to the checkpoint with families number one, two, and three for the real-life posada.

We gathered. We prayed. We wept, some of us. And then we walked in the usual, solemn silence to the checkpoint, where the adults said, again and as always:

> *We are Mexicans*
> *seeking your protection.*
> *Let us in, let us in!*

And the Border Patrol officers responded:

> *We have no room.*
> *We are full.*
> *Go away! Go away!*

We settled in to wait, then. But disturbed by the symbol-clash of realities every bit as much as I was, the bishop could not seem to wait that night. Visibly distressed but trying to bury it, he smiled gently and then leaned toward Lee and said quietly, "I'm going to go talk to them." Then he walked through the checkpoint and down the bridge to the US Border Patrol office at its base.

Ten minutes later those three holy families were through.

Grounded again by this small glimmer of hope, the bishop, canon, and I returned to the street to offer a faded farewell. At the base of the bridge, a man—not a member of the community but a passerby, a stranger—reached out to ask the bishop for a blessing, which, of course, he gave. Then the man, elderly, shrunken, dressed in the kind of baggy suit that suggests poverty rather than wealth, said, "Señor Obispo, thank you. Really, thank you. I can see that you are a truly humble man." This took the bishop utterly by surprise. "Humble?" he said, gesturing to his cassock and his cummerbund, before adding without even knowing what he was saying, "In all this!?!"

32

ON JANUARY 3, a group of men, all strangers, burst into the camp by the bridge next to ours and threatened to burn everything down if the community there didn't pack up and leave. It was dark, and the men swaggered fearlessly through the camp, all fortified certainty, and by the next morning, the camp at Puente Libre was empty.

Some families fled back into Mexico, apparently, but many—122, according to the newspaper—charged across the Rio Grande en masse instead. And when they were arrested on American soil, the United States allowed them to request asylum.

Officials on the Mexican side of the border found this last part enraging. Why would the US government reward those who broke the law by charging across the border, even as they continued to punish those who'd spent months trying to access the asylum process legally by approaching the checkpoints, day after day, asking politely to come in?

In an attempt to regain a semblance of control, these same officials—possibly in partnership with the United States, possibly not, who knows?—changed their approach to the people in the remaining two camps in Juárez. From then on, they insisted, Mexican citizens would no longer be allowed to seek asylum from the States on their own. They knew the communities had made their own lists, the officials said. And they knew, too, that these lists had worked. But not anymore. Now there would be only one list, the one run by the government, and only those officially registered on it would be recognized by officers at the checkpoints.

The very next day, men and women in uniform began visiting our street. They held clipboards thick with checklists and repeated over and over to the gathered crowds that only those on their list would be allowed to request asylum at the checkpoints. There would be no more locally run lists, the uniformed officials repeated. And no more going up the bridge on their own. If they did, they would be ignored. And sent back. And told only what they were being told now: that from then on, only those asylum seekers accompanied by representatives of the Instituto Nacional de Migración would be processed by the United States.

This was a huge shift in policy. While some of the more recently arrived families quietly made their way to the government-run office where they'd been told they should add themselves to the official list, most on the street remained suspicious and kept their distance. Who were the men who threatened to burn down the camp at Puente Libre? they kept asking. And what would happen to the families who charged across the river? And why was all this happening now? And most of all, who had what to gain? Who won through all this?

Tempers were growing short, and tensions were running high. People were so fearful that groups of similarly empowered thugs might come to our own camp that several families left the street that evening, crowding into tiny rooms with hourly rates until the following day, when they emerged again and began packing up the things in their tents.

No group of plain-clothed irregulars ever turned up, though. Instead, a large group of heavily armed, uniformed police pulled onto the street in pickups the following day, threatening to disperse the community if families with children didn't leave immediately.

It had been coming, this kind of pressure. The park by the Puente Libre had, by then, been completely cleared. There were pictures of it in the newspaper, empty but for a scrap or two of clothing left flapping from branches, and not a single person anywhere in sight. Gathering to look at these images in a single, shared newspaper, people from our camp huddled together by the chiclet stand, taut and watchful, and tried to figure out what to do. Options were quietly discussed later at the afternoon meeting as well. But in part because the community's own list had so suddenly—and so completely—lost its power, less than half of the community attended.

Most of the more recent arrivals had already signed on to the government-run list and had returned to the street with numbers they could track on an official members-only Facebook group. While Gerardo and Otilio and Yuritzi continued to parse their options, these newcomers stood apart in groups of two or three, bent over their phones, checking the page and then checking again, and again, waiting for numbers to post.

I left the street late that night and then prowled around the apartment, taut and watchful myself. Just before 11:00 p.m., a message came through on the community group chat: officials were back on the street.

"They're coming back tomorrow and if they find anyone here they will bring us to jail," Gerardo texted.

"Why?" Joselin asked.

"Because the children will die of the cold they say."

I made a plan to meet with the leaders first thing in the morning, then tried to pray, then tried to sleep. But it was too comfortable in my safe bed, in my safe neighborhood, in my safe city, and neither prayer nor sleep would come.

33

THE POLICE RETURNED at 10:00 a.m. in the morning on January 7 and told everyone that if they were still there in an hour, they would arrest the parents and send the children "out of state." I'd been standing by the bus stop with Yuritzi when the white pickup truck pulled onto the block, and as people began to gather around, I turned on my phone to record what was said. Here's part of it:

> Police Officer: *I've already told you what we will do if we find children, or minors of any kind, here when we come back. All we are doing is responding to a crime. That crime is neglect. And I have to tell you that in this case—especially at night when the temperatures go down—you are all certainly guilty of this. What we are going to do right now is make a census of the entire community here. You tell us how many children you have. Clear? Anyone have any questions?*
> Otilio: *Sir, we do not want any trouble and certainly do not intend to commit any crimes.*
> Police Officer: *We will see . . .*

Tania Guerrero sent a list of shelters that might make room, but no one would go. They didn't know these places, and they didn't trust them, Yuritzi said. "If you suggest a place you know, Cristi, we will go there—but only there," she said.

So that is what we did. I texted an Anglican priest, Hector, who had been rehabbing his parish hall to make it into a migrant shelter, and asked if he had any space.

"Yes," he texted back, almost immediately.

"How many beds?"

"About 130," he wrote.

When I shared the news that there was lots of room at Espíritu Santo Church, over in the Granjero district, Joselin wrote *Albergue Espíritu Santo* across the top of a piece of lined paper, which she clipped on to a board and circulated as a sign-up sheet. Ninety-two people signed up, though in the end only forty-five came.

No one was certain at that point that the cops would even come back. Thinking that routine would be good for the kids, we gathered them all for class at two as usual. Cynta, as always, had a lesson prepared, one that was good and instructive and fun. But we didn't get to finish it.

About forty-five minutes in, one of the parents came and whispered in my ear that we should speed things along. "Garbage trucks have arrived on the street," she said. "Also many officials."

Struggling to be calm, we wrapped things up as quickly as we could without alarming the kids and then headed back to the street via the shiny red bridge as always, climbing the metal steps up and then down with the repeated instruction not to run. Then—

Chaos.

Garbage trucks, pickup trucks, vans and white cars with flashing lights and official seals on the doors blocked both entrances to the street, which was already choked with uniformed officials. The press was there too. After so many months of nothing, writers and photographers carrying heavy black cameras like weapons were scrambling up and down the street as if it were a battlefield. Parents shouted at kids, *Fetch the backpack! Take the baby! Hold this!* as they dragged oversized blankets and piles of clothes and inflatable mattresses out from their tiny tents. I put my collar on, then borrowed a cart from Cynta and helped move people's gear to the pickup truck that was gathering the belongings of those heading for the shelter.

Behind us, in a weird and monstrous kind of slow motion, the munching chewing tearing of the garbage trucks echoed down the street as they consumed tents thrown in whole by yet more uniformed men—these ones in red—along with blankets and mats and toys and shoes. The knowledge that whatever was left would be consumed in this way slowed things down even as it speeded things up. There weren't enough bags to stuff things in. There wasn't enough time.

I lent the cart to Juan José, a single father of four who was struggling to transport all that remained of his family's possessions to a nearby hourly hotel, then walked up and down the street making sure the kids had at least one toy they cared about with them "Yes, I have my doll and her little stroller" (Ylani). "I have my cars" (Alejandro). "I have him!" pointing to a cuddly green dinosaur tucked under his arm (Dylan).

And through it all: the ravenous garbage trucks stretched open their foul mouths, consuming, consuming. And photographers peered into tents, shooting and shooting. And teenaged girls did all they could to keep their backs turned as they packed up their stuff, as if they were getting undressed, which of course they were. "Why are they taking photos?" Joselin's daughter kept asking through tears. "Why won't they leave us alone?"

At one point an official asked if I could help with the homeless American couple who had been staying in a tent the community had lent them for two or three days. Thanking God there was something I actually knew how to do, I headed over to their tent by the defunct public payphones and offered the guy twenty pesos if he would pack up and go. He said sure, twenty pesos would do it for him, but he couldn't vouch for his girlfriend. This remained his position until I upped the offer to fifty—and that was when the screaming started.

A young girl, three or four years old, in a fresh white dress was sitting straight-backed in the middle of the street in a state of pure panic, screaming, *Mami! Mami! Mami!* as she scanned the street back and forth, clutching a tiny, transparent plastic bag and pushing away anyone who came near her with all of her strength. Her mother had left her with a friend while she went to find a room, that friend told us now, and since she'd gone, the familiar street had morphed into this vortex of noise and fear and movement: the crunching of garbage trucks, the flashing of armored pickups, the squawking of radios and shouted instructions and guns and soldiers and cops and human rights workers and the press with their cameras pointing, getting too close, insisting. And through it all this tiny girl in white screaming, *Mami! Mami! Mami! Mami!*

Tania Guerrero was there by then, and the only thing she and I could do for the little one was sit down next to her on the ground, not too close or she'd lunge at us but close enough to keep her safe. "Mami! Mami! Mami! Mami!" she screamed, tearless now. "Mami! Mami! Mami!" until Tania—who for almost a year had spent every day of every week of every month listening to stories of human rights abuses so terrible she hardly ever shared them—started to weep.

The street was emptying out by then. Some people in the community fled to nearby churches, others slipped away to cheap hotels with hourly rates, and about fifty made their way to the bus heading out for the shelter at Espíritu Santo. Climbing onto the bus myself, I was followed by a photographer, who leaned into the space filled with families in flight yet again and started shooting. Alejandro's father, Otilio, waved his hands and told him to stop taking photographs of his family. But the photographer only leaned in closer. I leaped up and blocked his lens with the flat of my hand then, and was grateful (blessed relief!) when he turned his anger on me. Overwhelmed by the most active and urgent kind of powerlessness I have ever experienced, I shouted right back when he started shouting at me, until Otilio and another father came barreling down the aisle toward him, and he finally got off the bus. It was, truly, a horror. All of it.

Thank God then for the sturdy white structure of Espíritu Santo. Inside, the large parish hall turned shelter was still very basic: chairs lining the walls, a group of rectangular tables by the kitchen, and most everything covered in dust. But at least the community was together. And safe. And when a number of kids came up to me, dipping into the intimacy we shared when I'd look at their work at the end of class, and asked if I would teach class *here* tomorrow, I said, "What do you think? Of course!" And then I went home because I was good for nothing after that.

34

THE WEIRD STILLNESS of the street the following morning was almost as much of a shock as the chaos had been the day before. Except for a few frayed scraps of rope still knotted to the fence next to the bus stop, there was no sign that anyone had ever lived there. Like a clever set change, one reality had simply been swapped out for another. The emptiness there now was surreal. And disorienting. And heartbreaking.

Jaime the windshield washer was the only person there I knew, but he was drunk and floridly despairing, and he ended up leaning on a friend's shoulder and weaving down Juárez Ave weeping, looking for something to make himself feel better and promising to come back later. I walked over to the DIF building where we'd had class, crossing not on the shiny red metal walkway but through the traffic like any other normal person, crossing a normal street, on a normal day, trying to remember to breathe.

Cynta and Crystal joined me later in the Red Cross storage closet. We sorted a few books, salvaged a few crayons, and stuffed packs of Popsicle sticks and bottles of glue and tubes of glitter and tubs of safety scissors and construction paper into a cart. Then we headed over to Espíritu Santo with Lee in his car.

Cynta, Crystal, and I cleared a small space in the back corner of the parish hall to make a little room for class. We hauled chairs, dragged tables, swept and mopped the floor, and then laid down the seven-by-five-foot rug I'd lugged across the bridge earlier. But the kids were not able to sit still for class that day—and neither, honestly, were we. So we went out into the big concrete yard instead and drew on the ground with sidewalk chalk left over from before it was outlawed by parents on the street. Then we blew bubbles and watched as, delicate and fleeting, they floated up and over the church, riding currents we couldn't see, beautiful but critically insubstantial—designed, it seemed, to burst.

The truth is that I'd felt nothing when the pickups and police cars and giant garbage trucks rolled onto the street. Nothing when young Gloria helped to empty her family's tent, in her hampered way, determined to keep her back to the street. Nothing when Joselin finally screamed at her, "Move, daughter! What is wrong with you?" Nothing as families scrambled to stuff splitting garbage bags with all that was left from their lives. Nothing, even, as I sat next to the tiny girl in white who screamed and screamed and screamed for her mother on the street.

Later, though, it was different. Later I felt rage: at the US government and the Mexican government. And at all the various agencies with their color-coded uniforms. And at the church in the States too. Because, honestly, where were they?

Back in El Paso, after a short trip to the DIF and an even shorter one to lead a class and see what folks in the shelter most needed, I watched a video someone sent me of a press conference given by the mayor of Juárez. The community had been forcibly thrown off the street, I learned, because President Andrés Manuel López Obrador would be arriving for a tour of the city in a few days' time, and no one wanted to be embarrassed by the sight of Mexicans seeking asylum in the United States.

The mayor repeatedly denied that the two events were linked. But he also denied that any kind of threats had been made against the community, insisting that everyone left the street only because they wanted to. I had been there, though, and had heard the threats. For once, I knew exactly what had happened.

Ever since I'd arrived, I'd been trying to navigate the layers of reality that clashed and shattered each other on the border by enlarging my ability to hold contradictory truths together. Reality was multiple, I'd concluded. And malleable. Now, however, listening to the mayor, I was forced to correct myself again. It was not reality itself but only *interpretations* of reality that multiplied, burying the facts in obfuscation and lies, even as those same facts remained there, underneath all the layers, hidden perhaps (and perhaps even forever) but present nonetheless, both singular and real.

Welcome to the world of the border, a clear voice in my head said then. Also: Congratulations, Tina, you have finally arrived.

Every morning for the next week or so, I spent more than an hour in prayer, desperately trying to find some sense of connection, or strength, or peace. But every morning I failed. The two images of Jesus on my makeshift altar remained flat and distant; the candle flickered, not bright enough to light anything; and the photos of my sons were too painful even to look at. Only the marble from the homeless community in Boston, the one that looked like a globe, held any power to relieve, and I started to carry it in my pocket wherever I went, reaching for it when I felt overcome, or lost, or like I might cry.

I headed over to Juárez every day, too, of course, traveling first to the shelter where we continued to offer classes, after which I sat around with the women in the corner of the room closest to the kitchen, helping with paperwork, and drinking coffee, and finding fresh clothes for the kids. Then I'd cross town to the DIF to check in with the families waiting outside in the parking lot for updates on the list.

One afternoon that week—I no longer remember which one—Yuritzi led me by the arm across the parking lot to a bench where yet another newly returned mom was sitting alone. She needed help retrieving some items not yet returned by Border Patrol, Yuritzi told me, and I was grateful for the chance to do something useful.

It took a while for the mother to locate the exact piece of paper she needed from her beat-up pink and silver backpack, and when she finally found it, she waved it in the air like a winning raffle ticket. As we walked up to the bridge, she said, "Thank you, Cristi. Now I will be able to collect my daughter's unicorn."

"Your daughter's unicorn?" I checked, assuming I'd misunderstood.

"Yes. She loves that unicorn so much. Ever since the officials took it away, I've been praying they'd let me reclaim it. Now I will bring at least this back to her."

For a moment or two, I allowed myself to imagine what the Border Patrol storage area would look like if they kept and labeled and then carefully stored cuddly pink unicorns and green dinosaurs and little hard-headed dolls with their strollers, and I prayed for a world where such things happened. I didn't have the heart to tell her how unlikely this was, though. She still had five or ten minutes before she'd have to find out, I reasoned. Why take that from her? This wasn't very logical, I knew, or even particularly pastoral. But those first days after what I came to think of simply as The Destruction, all I could manage were little half-measures like this, ambivalent gestures, wilted actions rooted in the ash of despair.

At least families were continuing to get through, though. I needed to try and remember this. Everyone from the street—including Yuritzi, who I'd had to walk over to DIF to make sure she went—now had a numbered place on the government-run list. This meant that instead of passing through the turnstiles and walking silently up to the checkpoint and back every two hours, all people had to do was check their phones. And for hours each day, this is what they did: standing alone in the parking lot at DIF, or in small groups, heads bent over their phones as if in prayer, they clicked refresh over and over and over and over, waiting for updates, waiting for word.

Do I still need to mention that most of those being let in were being returned as well? Every day three or four families made their way back across the bridge on foot, telltale transparent bags in their hands, heads hung low. There was no more rational or comprehensible pattern as to who got through and who didn't than there had ever been. A family headed by two sisters, Paulina and Maura, who'd lived for months in the large green tent at the far end of the street, was divided right down the middle. One sister and her two kids were returned; the other, with her three, let through. Paulina and Maura shared the same case. The same story. The same relatives, reduced now to the same horror and blood. And nowhere was there anyone who could say why one got through and the other did not.

35

TEN DAYS LATER, about thirty-five people still remained at Espíritu Santo. A few were at a Baptist church downtown, and many more were living scattered among the cheapest hotels up close to the bridge, three or four families to a room. But without the structure and the leadership and the very real togetherness required for survival on the street, the community had begun to fracture.

One morning, just a few days in, a wave of texts from the shelter flooded my phone: A man had been interrupted in the beating of his wife by three children. Two mothers had left their kids at the shelter to go get a beer (and who wouldn't want a beer, I couldn't help thinking—who wouldn't?). And a guy named José had gotten drunk and then become so rude to Padre Hector that he threw him out and submitted a full written complaint to the authorities.

A handful of kids continued to gather at the shelter each day for class, and we did our best to keep up. We taught about red being for balls, and yellow being for sunshine, and green being for grass, but Cynta had already told me that she wouldn't be able to keep coming. The church was about twenty-five minutes from the border by car, and her husband, always nervous about her being in what was, after all, the fifth most dangerous city in the world, preferred she not travel so deep into Juárez. Crystal couldn't come either because she couldn't get the extra time off work.

Thank God the retired principal, Kathy, was keen to keep coming two days a week. Doug, a former court stenographer from Brooklyn who'd been coming regularly to the street for months by then, was also willing to do what he could at the shelter and had even started talking about buying a van. And soon enough, others stepped up to fill in the gaps. The Lutheran pastor of the El Paso church where I'd been worshipping on Sundays began to help with class once a week, and because of her we all got to spend an afternoon making crocodiles out of pipe cleaners and decorated popsicle sticks. Except a boy named Daniel. He made a creature with a tongue-depressor body half wrapped in green, four popsicle-stick arms sticking out from each side, and a googly-eyed face topped by a halo of brilliant gold feathers. When I asked him to tell me about his creation, he said, looking at me as if I should already know, "Es el ángel del Señor." It is the angel of the Lord.

Then he added quietly, as if to himself, "For this reason, no one can destroy him."

I called endless Ubers from the bridge to the shelter and tried not to worry as they took different, circuitous routes through the city to get there. On my way there one afternoon, we drove so far out that we passed a sprawling great cattle ranch, all mud and corrugated barns and cows and stench. I eyed the door handle closest to me, wondering whether it was locked and what it would take for me to propel myself through it if it wasn't. I was wide awake in the back of that car.

Most of the rest of the time, though, the muffled quality of my attention remained. I tried but could not will it away.

Interviewing had finally started for the new border chaplaincy position the diocese and I had created, and we had a couple of promising applicants. But after the destruction and dispersal of the community by the bridge, I felt sure my worn-out disengagement would be visible over Zoom. Worried about putting candidates off, I left most of the questions to Lee.

The inadequacy of my efforts seemed only to be growing. The appalling and infinitesimal tininess of what I was doing—walking across the bridge, sitting in an Uber, organizing books in plastic milk crates, playing music, cutting out little rabbits and pigs and trees for a mural—was making me, quite literally, sick. And through it all, families were returned, and returned, and returned. On January 14, my birthday, I watched as one family from the street was called to go through just as another was returned. This surreal intersection of one family's past with another family's future was too much for the parents, who nodded politely to each other but didn't speak. Their daughters were different, though. Yelping in recognition, they flung themselves into each other's arms like high school kids after a long summer break and then clung to each other: one in a gray detention-issue sweatshirt, the other in her own clothes, each still a very real part of the other's notion of home.

Just a few minutes later, two more families in gray walked into the parking lot of the DIF, deflated, exhausted, and despairing, and I was struck again, physically it felt like, by the weight of suffering so many had gone through only to land right back where they started—except worse. Because the behind-the-scenes possibility of change that had for so long sustained them—the hidden, hardly-ever-checked-in-on hope, like a tiny firefly glowing bright—had now been extinguished.

This was what the violence, and the terror, and the upheaval of flight, and the camping out on the street, and the eventual imprisonment like criminals led to: the parking lot of the DIF, where the only thing you had left—apart from your children, thanks be to God, and your freedom, which you would never again take for granted—was the question: what now?

36

WHAT NOW?

37

SLEEP WOULDN'T COME and wouldn't come and wouldn't come. I wandered around all day, pretending to be awake but actually asleep. Five minutes after tuning in to listen to the Scripture of the day, for example, I forgot what it was. I listened but did not hear. When I did sleep, I dreamed. And every dream ended with the same looping image: two huge, heavy, and course-gritted millstones with *US* and *Mexico* scraped into their sides, turning, turning. And between them, the poor—by whom I mean the people already persecuted and hounded and chased—were being ground, like maize, into dust.

Only when I was with the kids did anything make any sense. Some of those I'd grown closest to had gotten through, and every day they remained absent, my hope for them grew. Both Dylan and Alejandro had crossed, I reminded myself when I needed a boost. Alejandro, who'd told me proudly that he wanted to be a lawyer to "help people like us," had crossed with his father, Otilio, and his mother, Elizabeth, and who knew what his life might become if they managed to enroll him in a school system where someone might recognize his giftedness?

Alejandro's best friend, the ever-riotous Dylan, had crossed, too, on the very same day. I'd tried to catch a glimpse of them before they were escorted up the bridge, charging back to the DIF from the shelter as soon as I could after class. But they'd left by the time I got there, and I had to settle for a series of rushed messages over WhatsApp instead. "God bless you!" I wrote. And they wrote me back lines and lines and lines of smiley, sunglassed faces.

I knew their chances of being allowed to stay in the United States were so slight as to be negligible at that point. But a sliver of hope was better than no hope at all, and as I made my way to the shelter each day and prepared for class, I clung to it.

Then, halfway through a daylong trauma and resiliency training I'd registered for months before, I received a text from Alejandro's dad. Like so many others, their request for asylum had been denied, and after six long days and five long nights in detention, the family had been summarily returned. Otilio sent a photo of Alejandro, and it took my breath away. His skin was gray, and he was thin and so exhausted that he looked more like an old man than a young boy. He was blowing me a kiss in the photo, and I could just make out the bent tip of the finger he used to trace words out with when he read. This was how I was certain it was him. Honestly, he would have been unrecognizable otherwise. Less than a shadow of his regular self, it looked almost as if his spirit had left him. He was limp. Almost dead looking. But he was not dead; I had to keep telling myself this. Alejandro was not dead.

I tried to focus again on the training, but I lasted only twenty more minutes. I had a fierce headache suddenly and was so exhausted I could barely sit up. During a break, I slipped out of a door in the back and went straight to bed.

The fever that came then lasted three days. I went to the doctor, took a course of antibiotics that didn't work, spent six additional days in bed, and then returned to urgent care, where I was told I still had an infection in my respiratory tract and also in each of my ears. Both listless and restless, I was unable to cross back into Juárez—and also unable not to.

I spent hours in bed every day, looking at photos and trying to pray. Filled to bursting with grief—and with anger—I sent emails to friends back in Boston with the same three photos in each: Daniel, peering out of a house made of blocks. Juliana, on a green plastic tricycle. Alejandro (with one shoelace undone) about ten minutes before the street community was forcibly displaced.

"They are real, you know," I wrote in each message. "Flesh-and-blood kids, just like yours and mine."

38

A FULL WEEK later, the infection in my lungs had finally gone, but both ears were still full of liquid, which prevented me from hearing well all the time and sometimes from hearing at all. I was stunned by how accurately my body was reflecting my heart. How could it be that both physically and emotionally I could no longer hear? Occasionally, a person's voice still managed to break through. But not often. And rarely anyone other than a child.

I'd felt this way only once before. Two decades earlier, when I'd struggled to finish a book about women in prison, the horrors of the criminal justice system had flooded me just like this, and I'd been swamped for months by great waves of inexpressible rage and sorrow and grief. Had I simply come full circle, then? This was what I wondered. Or was it, at least, more of a spiral than a circle? I was in a similar state, for sure, full to bursting with the suffering of others and with my own sense of lostness and powerlessness and unmet responsibility in the face of it. But I'd spent most of the time since then struggling with, following and failing to follow, and loving and failing to love He-who-Himself-is-love, Jesus. And there was at least a chance that I could choose to respond differently now.

Twenty years before, I'd known nothing about this man-who-was-God-who-was-love and had only my own will, faltering and wayward and undisciplined, to fall back on. Now, of course, I was still faltering and wayward and undisciplined. But I was also more . . . what was the word? Diversified? Because I had at least the beginnings of the muscles of faith, by which I mean the muscles that might lead to trust, if not trust itself; and to love, if not love itself; and to surrender and self-forgetting, if not surrender and self-forgetting themselves.

I was both the same and changed then, both old and new—and so, at the same time, neither. Searching for a present I could make sense of, while still rooted in the too recent, stripped away past, I was stuck in a place in between. And it was small there, and cramped, and there didn't seem to be enough air to breathe.

I tried to keep doing the things I was supposed to be doing. But I didn't yet have the physical strength, which threw me back again to myself, and to the silence of my own heart, and to—yes—Jesus's presence there, in me even then, when there was no sensible proof of that presence at all. Jesus with and in and through me, silently welcoming, and strengthening and longing . . . yes, even then, longing for me.

It was almost impossible to believe this.

But it was true.

39

I RETURNED TO Juárez just in time for Valentine's Day. Día de Amor y Amistad, they call it in Mexico: Day of Love and Friendship. I went straight to Espíritu Santo with Lee and a wonderful young woman named Ana, who was interviewing for the chaplaincy job. I'd brought plenty of special purple, red, and orange foamy sheets to make cards with, along with glitter and glue, and the class went well until it was interrupted by the entrance of an older woman, talking fast.

She was just out of detention, we could tell because of her gray sweatshirt and gray sweatpants, and she spoke so quickly that no one except ten-year-old Brian could follow her. Brian was alone that day. His older brother was off downtown someplace with his new girlfriend. ("They are *friends!*" he insisted when another kid called them novios. "Just *friends!*" "Okay," the other kid said. "I only called them novios because they *kiss* each other.")

Left behind and feeling a little hurt and lonely, Brian seemed grateful for the distraction, and he concentrated hard as the terrified woman spoke all in a jumble. She was looking for her family, he told us—"For her daughter, I think, and her niece?" The woman nodded energetically at this, but she was so rattled that she wouldn't say their names, and we had no way of knowing who they were. Did she have a photo? No, no, she said. Sitting next to her on the bench, attentive as an altar boy, Brian asked a few questions, quietly, only to her. Then he leaped up: "I think I know who they are—I think they arrived last night!" he announced. "I'm going to see if they are upstairs."

The old woman's husband had stepped shakily into the room by then. He was an elderly, dignified man from the countryside, with a weatherworn face and bright white, close-cropped hair. Together they followed Brian slowly up the fire escape stairs to the dorms. Several minutes later Brian returned and told Ana and me that the family had reunited and, matter-of-factly, that the old lady was crying. Then he tucked into a bowl of Valentine's Day Hershey's Kisses.

"I've been fantastically helpful. I figured it out," he said, repeating words I'd just told him, as he paid himself with a pocketful of two (glance at me), three (glance at me), four Hershey's Kisses.

Later the husband came down to smoke a cigarette outside in the sun. He spoke in details instead of narratives, in fragments. I listened as closely as I could and started to understand that four young men in his family had been murdered in the last seventy-two hours. Stabbed and shot. Right next to their ranch. *Pam-pam-pam-pam-pam.* In their car. Together. The wetness of the blood. The places that it pooled. The way the driver's head looked. The two in the back.

He, his wife, and twenty-eight other members of their extended family had arrived in Juárez two nights before and went straight to the border to ask the United States for protection. The two grandparents were let straight in. Only now, fewer than forty-eight hours later, here they were again: their request for asylum formally denied.

It was the same old story. Here's part of the transcript:

What will you do if you fail to gain asylum?
I will go back to Mexico.
Are you afraid to live in another area of Mexico?
No.
Do you know what asylum means?
No. I have heard it can make you more secure, but I do not really know.

These answers alone were enough to fail the interview and change the life of his family forever. But what else could he say? If he was denied access to the United States, where else could this elderly and dignified rural worker go except back to Mexico? Besides, he was unable to think clearly even then, and his wife even less so.

And tell me: who *would* be able to speak clearly under circumstances like this? Would you? I mean, if you'd just seen four of your sons and nephews in a bloodbath of a car where they had been stabbed and then shot outside your home, and then spent the night running with your spouse, who was even more undone than you, and twenty-eight other members of your family, who you'd gathered up and kept together: would *you* be able to clearly and precisely answer the questions a uniformed officer asks you in the foreign language of a foreign country during something you have no idea is even called a credible fear interview?

I still knew so little, but I knew at least that no provision was any longer being made for any of this. There were set questions and set answers, and if an asylum seeker answered the set questions in ways that did not directly fulfill the requirements, they failed and were sent back to what very well may be their death.

This is just the way it was—and is still. Every day. Over and over again.

The old man was still talking, interrupting himself now to rage about "the officials over there." "They kept asking us if we were delinquents," he said, leaning forward in his chair, incensed. "*We!* I am a law-abiding man, a hard worker all my life. We have run through the night without even burying our sons. But all they want to know is 'Have you ever been convicted of a crime? Have you spent time in prison?' Even of the women they asked this! Even of my wife!" and I was struck again by how much pride and honor and steadfastness became invisible in the whittled-down world of border detention.

Brian came outside then and sat next to the old man on a step in the shade, which meant I had a decision to make. I could continue to witness to the old man's grief and rage or focus on Brian and get him away from the too-bright glimpses of horror the old man was conjuring. "With a knife, they cut him from here to here," he was saying now, slicing a line from the base of his neck to his groin. I decided to go with Brian.

"I'm so bored," he said, scuffing the edge of his sneaker against the leg of a table when we got back inside.

"No, Brian, you are not bored," I said gently. "But let's make a card for your mama. Or for your brother—or your uncle in the States, maybe." When he didn't respond to that, I said, "You can choose the music," which shifted things.

"Ozuna!" he decreed and did a little macho dance move in imitation of his favorite Puerto Rican trap star before pulling out a sheet of purple fomi and drawing a wobbly heart.

40

IT WAS TIME for me to go. The only family from the street left by then was Joselin's. One family more and then . . . well, and then everyone from the community on the street would at least have been able to do what they should have been able to do the minute they arrived in Juárez: ask the United States for protection.

It felt okay, suddenly, to leave. The diocese had hired Ana to continue to work with asylum seekers on both sides of the border, and they had raised funds to keep this work going for at least one full year, which, at least, felt like something. And the people who'd started this something—the families from Zacatecas and Guerrero and Michoacán who had shaped and formed and created it—had by then dispersed. Soon I would join them.

Lee organized a goodbye party at the shelter, and it seemed right to use my departure as an excuse, at least, for a celebration. In addition to Brian and Nico and Daniel and a handful of other kids and their families, Lee was there, and Ana, who would take over from me when I left, and Kathy, of course, and Doug. After taking several votes in class the week before, the kids had finally agreed that pizza and a movie was the way to go, and I brought candy and beads and shiny colored cardboard crowns that a friend from Boston had sent for the occasion. Placing crowns on the kids' heads before settling in to watch *Aladdin* felt so obviously sacramental, so clearly an instance of making the invisible visible, that I nearly burst into tears. I only kept it together because of the crazy-making back-and-forth flow of kids wanting to change the color of their crown: Can I have a silver one, Cristi? Oh *please*, can I change this one for a purple? But green is my *favorite color*!

Joselin and her family had gotten through that morning. This meant the community from the street had now, finally and completely, dispersed. Some were out, on the other side "over there," beginning new lives in South Dakota and Illinois and West Virginia and Kansas and North Carolina and Iowa and Idaho and Missouri. Some were still in detention—in El Paso or New Mexico, mostly, but a few in places as far away as Louisiana and Alabama. And many others, of course, were back in Mexico, forced to start all over again under uncertain circumstances, in new places, with diminished connections away from the border and whatever promise it once held. In a way, my work was done, which only showed how tiny it was in the first place.

My tiny work, such as it was then: done. Even as new people arrived every day, carried by streams of hope for safety and newness of life in the States, only to be stopped in the stormy ocean of suffering both created and bound by the wall. It was hard to get my head around.

Back in the shelter, though, *Aladdin* was a hit. One by one the adults were drawn to the brightness of the screen and the laughter of the kids, and we pulled up extra chairs from across the room and offered popcorn and candy to everyone when the pizza was done. Sitting quietly by the wall, I watched as the kids crowded up front, along one of the church pews that framed the "theater," laughing and shouting encouragement to the young boy on the screen. Their crowns—crooked now mostly or pushed back high on their heads—glittered in the projector's light as they ate popcorn out of plastic cups and knocked back soda. When it was done, we all hugged and laughed and wept, and the kids gave me the handmade cards, stiff with glitter, that sit next to me as I write these words now.

Through it all, they had remained human. This much is clear.

But did we? Had I?

41

I PACKED. MADE and received phone calls with families who had gotten through and families who had been returned. I cried, and also failed to cry, both at the wrong time.

Before I left, I made one last visit to Juárez to see Alejandro's dad, Otilio. He'd moved into a room above the Michoacána ice cream store with another former leader from the street, Gerardo, who'd also been returned under HARP. The owner of the Michoacána gave them this space for free, and they were making almost enough to eat by helping out the vendors at the chiclet stand by the foot of the bridge.

Alejandro and his mom had already left on their long journey home by way of La Basílica de Nuestra Señora de la Salud, the Basilica of Our Lady of Health. This required a two-hundred-mile detour, but it was important, he said, to give thanks for the Virgin's protection during these difficult months.

Like so many others, Alejandro and his mother would return to their home state but not to their hometown, as it remained too dangerous for them there. They were hoping to stay with an aunt, but were uncertain whether this would work out.

Otilio wept when he told me this. Right there at the chiclet stand, twenty feet from the bridge, he wept, wiping the tears with the flats of his fingers so he could see again. He was trying to find another way to cross, he told me, though he didn't really want to anymore. He'd seen how it was over there, he said, and he'd rather stay home.

"Why don't you?" I asked.

"You have to understand, Cristi—I have big debts from all this," he said. "How else can I pay them?"

Other families from the street continued to be returned to Juárez regularly. Almost every day they crossed back down the bridge in gray, exhausted, close to despair, wanting only to find a place to rest and then later, perhaps, to figure out what was next. Otilio served as a kind of informal greeting committee, commiserating with them, suggesting cheap places to stay, offering directions, lending an ear to the horrors that were the same and also different from his own: a guard separating their family on the inside, a sister or a wife or a husband still locked up and now "lost" in the system, a child pushed, a parent sickened and separated from the rest.

But others made it through and then stayed, which at that point was almost as bad. Otilio knew he shouldn't feel this way, but it was just the truth, because it made no sense, he said. Try hard as he might, he could simply find no way to have it make any sense! Wasn't his case at least as bad as that of some of those who had crossed? Didn't the lives of the people he lost count? Didn't his own? And hadn't he spent, in addition to all this, months and months helping to take care of everyone on the street, making sure they were safe, and cared for, and able to rely on the integrity of their list?

"So many people have written to thank me," he said then. "Moisés and Antonia and Yuritzi all wrote. They all made it through, Cristi—look! Moisés even wrote me from work," he said, forcing a smile as he showed me a photo of a house under construction somewhere over there, on the other side, where he wasn't.

We walked to the market, shared some tacos, bought a pair of jeans and some sneakers to replace the orange foam Crocs the detention center had left him with, and then it was time to leave. I didn't want to cross the bridge back into the States so visibly, right there in front of Otilio, but he was needed at the chiclet stand, so I had no choice. We hugged. And wept. And then hugged again. And I felt him both looking and not looking at me as I put my coins into the turnstile, both connected and separate as I walked away.

Heading up the bridge for the last time, I struggled to keep it together. I hated that bridge. And I loved that bridge. And I had no idea in the world where the horror and the beauty of that bridge were leading any of us.

Then I remembered Daniel, the boy who made the Angel of the Lord out of popsicle sticks in class at Espíritu Santo. A round boy of eight, who had the kind of fanciful imagination that made him vulnerable to his peers, Daniel tended to play alone. The last time I'd seen him, he'd been working intently for almost an hour on a yellow chalk creation out in the yard. It was a giant scribble, really—a long, intricate line curling and twisting from one side of the tarmac to the other like a giant snail trail. When he was finally done, he announced that it was a treasure map. "Would you like to try and follow it?" he asked.

"I would," I said, quite certain.

"Good! Now, then," he said, tapping his bottom lip with the tips of his fingers as he surveyed the scene. "Where did it start? Ah, yes!" he finally remembered, "Right . . . over. . . . here."

I did my best to follow the scribbly line exactly, making my way along it slowly, carefully. As I tiptoed along, I became aware that Daniel was beaming at me from the edge of the yard like a miniature Buddha. Willing me along the right path, he blessed me on with his entire being, nodding when I made the tight and twisty turn underneath the basketball hoop hung by Doug and then again as I realized an error and stepped back to my left to correct it.

And his smile when I finally arrived at the square with an X in it, marking the treasure at the end of the line? Imagine Jesus when he finally receives you in his arms, only younger and rounder: full of pride and joy and celebration at my very delayed, often uncertain, and much-worried-about arrival.

I was—always and again—being saved by the little ones.

Thanks be to God.

EPILOGUE

LESS THAN TWENTY-FOUR hours after walking across the bridge from Juárez to El Paso for the very last time, I unlocked the front door of my house back in Boston and walked in. I remember nothing about the plane ride or the trip from the airport to my house. But I will never forget the first few minutes of being back in that space.

It was late afternoon, and the sun was streaming into the kitchen from the window by the stove, pooling in warm puddles on the edge of the worn kitchen table and the back of a chair, and sliding over the corner of the counter and across the curved wooden handle of the kettle. I was utterly stopped by this, astonished and taken aback by the scene's silent beauty. As slowly as I could, and as quietly, I put down my suitcase, unhitched my backpack, walked into the hushedness, and then reached out and touched the things one by one, naming them in a whisper as I went. Kitchen table, chair, kitchen counter, kettle.

Home, I thought.

Then I said it out loud: home.

A blast of the border's horror and grief blew through me then, and I was stricken by shame. But then, just as suddenly, that same shame dissolved. This was what everyone on the street was risking their lives for, I realized: the safe hush of a table, a chair, a kitchen counter, a kettle. They weren't things to be ignored, then, or walked past, or pushed away. They were, instead, the point: for the people pressed up against the border, for the men and women who lived on the streets of Boston, and also for me. We were all searching for home. We *are* all searching for home. And the chair and the table and the kettle, which would soon have steam dancing up from its spout, are and were, and, God willing, long will be a kind of home for me. This handful of familiar items glowing gently in a small room in a small house on a regular street where neighbors greet each other as if peace were the most normal thing in the world.

I thought I could rest then—exhale and regroup and begin to recover at least some of the energy and potential for connection I seemed to have lost. Six days later, though, COVID-19 shut down the country. And from that moment on, no one in Juárez—or anywhere along the southern side of the 1,951 miles of border—would be allowed to request asylum for any reason, for years.

A new protocol was quickly instituted to ensure this. Named Title 42, it allowed all newly arrived migrants, even asylum seekers on American soil, to be immediately expelled, without any due process at all. Title 42 was touted as a public health response to the pandemic threat. It was implemented, though, not by scientists but by the same people who'd put together HARP, and MPP before it, and metering before that: the Department of Homeland Security and the Oval Office. In fact, scientists from the Centers for Disease Control vociferously opposed its implementation, arguing, reasonably enough, that as long as our borders remained open to other kinds of travelers, there was no public health rationale at all for Title 42.

Despite this, however, the protocol remained, and tens of thousands of asylum seekers were turned back from checkpoints up and down the border during those first, worst months of the pandemic. With no place else to go, many of these men, women, and children hunkered down in makeshift camps similar to the one by the Paso del Norte bridge. It was impossible to maintain anything like safe social distancing under conditions like these, of course, and no one knows how many people contracted COVID-19 in the camps and died as a result. No one counted.

Title 42 finally expired during the spring of 2023 after multiple lawsuits challenged its legitimacy. Other measures were immediately put into effect to keep some of the world's most vulnerable people from accessing asylum in the States. Then, in the back-and-forth way of border politics, these measures were also rescinded. By the end of the year, more than 800,000 people requesting asylum had been allowed into the United States. Emergency shelters across the country started to fill with thousands of asylum seekers who were suddenly granted access to a system that couldn't grow in capacity fast enough, and the already yearslong backlogs in asylum hearings started to balloon. In 2024, an election year, the presence of so many asylum seekers across the country became a political liability. As a result—and once again—more newly restrictive measures were implemented at the border, and within months claims fell by more than 50 percent. Through it all, however, one thing remained constant: more than 85 percent of all asylum requests were ultimately denied.

It's a great irony that a country founded on immigration—a country that continues to proclaim, proudly, "Give me your tired, your poor, your huddled masses yearning to breathe free"—now formally welcomes fewer people who are "homeless and tempest tost" each year than any other developed country on earth.

I still don't like figures. They are, too often, too easy to skim. But just by way of a global sketch: as of June 2023, 110 million people across the world were in flight from their homes. Despite our politicians' frantic rhetoric about being overburdened and overrun by people seeking entrance to our country, almost 90 percent of these people in flight are hosted in low- and middle-income countries, including Iran (3.4 million), Turkey (3.4 million), Colombia (2.5 million), Uganda (1.5 million), and Pakistan (2.1 million).

The United States, by comparison, welcomed 60,014 refugees and granted asylum to just 17,692.

Something has to change.

This little book has been my attempt to do what small thing I can, both as a human being and as a priest, to spread the word. It is not nearly enough, I know. But that is almost always the case, almost all the time, with almost everything every one of us does. And contrary to the mores of our culture, which eschew and abhor limits of every kind, I continue to believe that acknowledgment of this fact can be generative. More and more it seems to me that "not nearly enough" is not a barrier to doing the work so much as a real place to start—and then to try to build on.

Of course, if our efforts seem, clearly, to be not nearly enough, that is largely because the facts on the ground seem, just as clearly, to be way too much. Too much to take in. Too much to read about sometimes even, and we swipe the page or switch the station and think, Later I will come back to it. Later I will let myself see.

But if you are reading this page, you have let yourself see, for at least several hours. And you have let yourself feel. And you have let yourself recognize, I hope, the truth and the power and the dignity and sanctity of so many of the people on the border.

Pope Francis, that great friend of people who have been displaced across the globe, has said, repeatedly, that in response to this crisis of forced migration, all we wealthier, more stably housed people need to do is listen to the stories of those who are suffering, that this listening is enough.

I'm not sure if this is true. I do believe, though, that the power these stories hold—which is to say the power that ignites and sustains and dwells deep within the hearts of every one of the people who are primarily affected by the brutality of our borders—has the potential to begin the process of healing for us all.

People on the move have a lot to teach the rest of us about what it means to be human, that's the thing. Forced to confront their own fear and vulnerability as they navigate levels of hardship many of the rest of us are protected from, they've learned more about their need for hope and help and peace than the rest of us—and so also more about how we might get there, one day, together.

But for us to learn, we must let them teach us. And to do that, we must first let go of our terrified attempts to remain powerful and secure and set apart from the fray. No number of walls—of brick or metal or comfort or privilege—will keep the suffering of the world at bay. It is simply impossible. We have a better chance of reducing the grief of the world by opening ourselves—even briefly—to its fullness, and then by daring to approach those who are most obviously suffering, fully aware of all we do not yet know and cannot yet see, and so wanting to learn and grow as much as to give.

If we are to have even a chance of making things better along our own borders, then, our task needs to involve as much listening and learning as it does practical work to alleviate whatever small part of the suffering we can. And not for the sake of migrants and asylum seekers only but also for ours. We are all reduced by keeping so much apart. And we are all impoverished. Because the truth of life revealed in the broken places—which is to say the truth of hope and of need and of love—is as essential to those of us who live in comfort as it is to those who do not. . . yet.

This isn't as easy as it sounds. Even if we do honestly desire to help make the world a better place, spending time with individuals is a slow, pitifully local way to do it. The truth is that I often felt useless walking over the bridge into Juárez every day, with no plan beyond class for the kids and, most days, a walk up to the checkpoint and its accompanying disempowering, deflating, sometimes enraging walk back down again. Why am I doing this? I'd ask. What is the point?

The questions still feel very real, even all this time later. And I find myself answering them—again!—the way I always did: because in this way I share at least a little in the suffering and real powerlessness of the people. And somehow leaning into that—the action itself, I mean, the *act* of leaning in—draws me into the power of God, which only those who know their own powerlessness seem to have access to. And with this power . . . what?

I was able to write this book, perhaps. And you have been able to read it. And from here: who knows?

One thing I am certain about: the border is everywhere in our country today—its effects and also its people. Families from the street by the Paso del Norte bridge are, right now, making lives in the big cities, small towns, and rural communities of every single state of this country. If you choose, it would be simple to find ways to connect with them. "But what good would that do?" I hear you say. "It is not enough." And I know, believe me I know how you feel! But then I remember: Not enough is better than nothing. Not enough, once accepted, keeps us going and leads us on. Not enough, in the end, draws us toward each other in love and awareness of our mutual need. And when that happens . . .

Well, when that happens, you will know.

ACKNOWLEDGMENTS

FOR ALMOST TWENTY years, the Brothers of the Society of Saint John the Evangelist have given me a home in which to pray, write, breathe, and become. Br. Curtis Almquist especially has been a generous mentor and friend, and this book would never have been possible without his prayers. Br. Dave Semmens and Fr. Peter Hinde, both of the Order of Carmelites, were also early and essential supporters, and a Carmelite Charity Grant helped me to begin it.

Deep gratitude also to Barney Karpfinger, who is—simply—the most steadfastly supportive and radically faithful agent imaginable, and to my editor at Broadleaf, Valerie Weaver-Zercher, whose care and intelligence improved these pages hugely. I hope always to work with them both.

I must also thank Meg Turner here, whose wisdom, patience, and loving restraint guide me still; Kathryn Geismar, who has shown me what it means to be faithful; Julia Slayton, who returns me to myself every time I see her; and Ann Steigerwald, who trusted me when I needed it most. The Calabresi-Oldshue family, Steve Bonsey, Elisabeth Keller, and Silvia Gosnell made my initial exploration of the border possible. Francisco Goldman, Jovi Montes Hernandez, Azalea, and Yoyo offered joyous and generous respite whenever I needed it, away from the fray in Mexico City. And every one of the Sánchez-DeCórdoba-Rathbone clan who, together, make up La Familia.

In Massachusetts, I must thank first the people of the MANNA community who, through no fault of their own, made me the priest that I am. Also Michael Attïas, Nina Calabresi, Arrington Chambliss, Leah Hager Cohen, Jessica Hedges, Jane O'Connor, Jennifer McCracken, and James Parker, who, together, make up the most wonderful chosen family a person could have; my daily writing partners Dave Woessner, Cora McCold, and Kate Glavin have been essential, too, as have been Pennie Curry and every one of the extraordinary people of Grace Church: an Episcopal Community in the Southern Berkshires.

In El Paso, I owe huge gratitude to the people of the Episcopal Diocese of the Rio Grande, especially Bishop Michael Hunn and Canon Lee Curtis, for their support of the work that became the Bridge Chaplaincy. Also Sister Bea and everyone from Annunciation House and Casa Vides, Dave Semmens, Henry Craver, Doug Winter, Sarah Guck, Cynta Torres, Kathy Jacks, and Diana Linden-Johnson.

In Juárez, Cristina Coronado, Sigrid Gonzalez, Tania Guerrero, Sandra Rodriguez, Peter Hinde, and Betty Campbell all taught me—through word and example—how to navigate life on the border with faith, perseverance, and joy.

Last, and most deeply of all, thank you, thank you, thank you to the extraordinary people—both adults and children—who formed and sustained the community by the Paso del Norte bridge. For reasons of safety and security, I have not been able to use their real names here. Nor, though I have surely tried, have I been able to express even half their beauty, courage, generosity, and grace.

RESOURCES

HERE IS A list of national organizations that work with asylum seekers on the border and in the communities they move to once they arrive.

- US Committee for Refugees and Immigrants, https://refugees.org
- World Relief, https://worldrelief.org
- HIAS, https://www.hias.org
- International Rescue Committee, www.rescue.org/
- Ethiopian Community Development Council, https://www.ecdcus.org/
- Global Refuge, https://www.globalrefuge.org/
- Catholic Legal Immigration Network, https://www.cliniclegal.org
- Church World Service, https://cwsglobal.org
- Episcopal Migration Ministries, https://episcopalmigrationministries.org/
- KIND, https://supportkind.org/

NOTES

Introduction
    Page 1: *Across the globe:* United Nations High Commission for Refugees, *Global Trends Report: World at War* (Geneva: UNHCR, June 2018).

Chapter 3
    Page 27: *Juárez was, in other words, a pretty rough place:* El Diario de Juárez, numerous articles 2019–20 including "El Año Mas Violento" (December 23, 2019), "Solo en 7 días del 2019 no hubo ejecutados" (January 1, 2020), other statistics (September 1, 2019, and May 8, 2019).

Chapter 15
    Page 114: *"But I know this":* Sandra Cisneros, *A House of My Own: Stories from My Life* (New York: Knopf, 2015), 38.

Chapter 17
    Page 125: *"Washington's idea of leadership":* Jeffrey Goldberg, "The Man Who Couldn't Take It Anymore," *Atlantic*, October 2019, https://www.theatlantic.com/magazine/archive/2019/10/james-mattis-trump/596665/.

Chapter 22
    Page 153: *Though the cords:* Lines adapted from Psalm 119, verses 61, 129, 150, 153, 158 (NRSV).

Chapter 25
>**Page 176:** ***"My mantra has persistently":*** Gus Bova, "In Nuevo Laredo, Trump's 'Remain in Mexico' Feels Chaotic and Dangerous," *Texas Observer*, July 31, 2019, https://www.texasobserver.org/in-nuevo-laredo-trumps-remain-in-mexico-program-feels-chaotic-and-dangerous/.

Chapter 33
>**Page 223:** ***Through it all:*** Eileen Sullivan, "Asylum in America, by the Numbers," *The New York Times*, November 21, 2023, https://www.nytimes.com/2023/11/21/us/politics/migrant-crisis-border-asylum.html.

Epilogue
>**Page 259:** ***But just by way:*** United Nations High Commission for Refugees, *Mid-Year Trends Report* (Geneva: UNHCR, June 2023).
>
>**Page 259:** ***Despite our politicians':*** United Nations High Commission for Refugees, *Mid-Year Trends Report* (Geneva: UNHCR, June 2023).
>
>**Page 260:** ***The United States, by comparison:*** "Programs," Migration Policy Institute, https://www.migrationpolicy.org/programs/data-hub/charts/us-refugee-resettlementin.
>
>**Page 260:** ***Something has to change:*** United Nations High Commission for Refugees, *Mid-Year Trends Report* (Geneva: UNHCR, June 2023).